LEARNING SALE PRICE RAISING STRATEGY

JOHN LOK

Made with ♥ on the Notion Press Platform
www.notionpress.com

Contents

Preface

Introduction

In our societies , any kinds of products or services must need to apply demand and supply economic theory to analyze whether the kind of product or service may be value to invent to sell or serve to their customers in consumer market, if the kind of product or service demand number is less, then it ought not to raise manufacturing number to avoid "low price " sale or if the kind of product demand number is more, then it ought raise manufacturing number to have enough number in order to raise " high price" sale to satisfy customers their needs to buy their products. However, whether your product or serive's demand number depends on supply number or your product or service's supply number depends on demand number in order to make ths sale price is reasonable high or low level and reasonable supply number valuation.
In my this book, I shall indicate some actual product or service social suitation to explain whether it is right time to these kinds of product or service of their sale price ought increase or demand in market demand and supply environment in order to avoid customers number reduce. Readers can learn sale price strategy of these sale cases studies.

Prologue

Contents

Chapter 10 Reasons of societal marketing orientation may help body shop to raise sale price

What is the difference between production orientation and societal marketing orientation and sales orientation to body shop ? p.191-200

Chapter 11 Reason of sales of ready meals in supermarket may help cooking food raise sale price

Case study change in the marketing environment on sales of ready meals to supermarket, such as Walt Mark strategy ? p.201-210

Chapter 12 online shopping sale price raising strategy

E-commerce how influences consumer behavioral changes to bring positive or better economy growth to the country?

How e-commerce influence the country's economic and consumer behavioral changes ?

How the E-commerce influences demand patterns ?

Factors Influencing E-Commerce Development Implications for the Developing Country consumer behavior ?

How to predict Consumer Behavior in the Retail Industry ?

What are Implications for Ecommerce in Developing Countries consumer shopping convenient need factor ?

What are the negative influences or impacts to influence the country's consumer behaviors when the country is encountering any kinds of death disease ? Why does death disease bring economic recession to the country when the country can not control the death disease to cause many people to die , when they are free to go to anywhere and the owning death disease people can contract any people , they have no death disease easily? p.211-230

Chapter 13 University school fee raising strategy

How can University campus location factor influence student choice?
Can online and hybrid courses will influence to university students to choose
the university to study? p.231-240

Chapter 14 Airport shopping sale price raising strategy

Can airport time consumption factor influence airport passenger shopping behavior ?

Can the country's airport service performance influence passengers consumption desire?

Every country cultural difference is different. How and why cultural difference has a real impact on tourist satisfaction and it can also influence to repeat travel?

How any why peer-to-peer accommdation can attract business tourisms to choose business tourism intention? What are the main internal and external factors to influence local tourist's domestic to
travelling choice behaviors and destination choice decision making?

Does every tourist individual driving behavior influence whose travel behavioral choice?

What are usually travel behaviors and attitudes to disabled tourists ?

Can web site online internet networking influence traveller individual behavior changes? p.241-255

Chapter 15 Disney ticket price increasing strategy

What strategy can solve long time queue to bring theme park entertainment industry visitors negative emotion ?

Can Disney short time knowledge management strategy solve long time queue entertainment waiting challenge to visitors ? p.256-266

CHAPTER ONE

Explaining supply and demand economic theory relationship

The difference between past and nowadays economists their demand and supply economic theory explanation?

The law of supply and demand defines the relationship between the price of a given good or product and the willingness of people to either buy or sell it. Generally, as the price of a good increases, people are willing to supply more and demand less. These economists had explained economic demand and supply theory as below:

Philosopher John Locke is credited with one of the earliest written descriptions of this economic principle in his 1691 publication, Some Considerations of the Consequences of the Lowering of Interest and the Raising of the Value of Money. Locke addressed the concept of supply and demand as part of a discussion about interest rates in 17th-century England. Many merchants wanted the government to lower the cap on interest rates charged by private lenders so that people could borrow more money and thus purchase more goods. Locke argued that the free-market economy should set rates because government regulation could have unintended consequences. If the lending industry were left alone, interest rates would regulate themselves, Locke wrote: "The price of any commodity rises or falls by the proportion of the number of buyers and sellers."

Sir James Steuart's Inquiry into the Principles of Political Economy, published in 1796, was the first known printed use of the term "supply and demand." When Steuart wrote his treatise on political economy, one of his main concerns was the impact of supply and demand on laborers.

Adam Smith dealt extensively with the topic in his 1776 epic economic work, The Wealth of Nations. Often referred to as the Father of Economics, Smith explained the concept of supply and demand as an "invisible hand" that naturally guides the economy. According to Smith, the invisible hand is the automatic pricing and distribution mechanisms in the economy. Smith described a society in which bakers and butchers provide products that individuals need and want, providing a supply that meets demand and developing an economy that benefits everyone. It is important to note that Smith's ideas haven't gone without critique over the years since his ideas were first published, though. Over time, his ideas have been added to in order to represent the changing times and include concepts such as marginal utility, comparative advantage, entrepreneurship, the time-preference theory of interest, and monetary theory.

One of Marshall's most important contributions to microeconomics was his introduction of the concept of price elasticity of demand, which examines how price changes affect demand. In theory, people buy less of a particular product if the price increases, but Marshall noted that in real life, this behavior was not always true. The prices of some goods can increase without reducing demand, which means their prices are inelastic. Inelastic goods tend to include items such as medication or food that consumers deem crucial to daily life. Marshall argued that supply and demand, costs of production, and price elasticity all work together.

Nowadays economists they explain demand and supply economic theory, they have some different to past economists whose explanation as below:

How Does Supply and Demand Work? The law of supply and demand is a theory that explains the interaction between the sellers of a resource and the buyers of that resource. Generally, as price increases, people are willing to supply more and demand less and vice versa when the price falls.

What does the bottom line mean. Despite the origins of the law of supply and demand beginning hundreds of years ago, it's still a topic frequently referenced and utilized today in economic theory and discussions. The theory has developed over time to accommodate recent technological and economical advancements, but the basic ideas of the theory remain largely the same.

Does demand depend on supply?

Supply and Demand Determine the Price of Goods and Quantities Produced and Consumed. Consumers may exhaust the available supply of a good by purchasing a given good or service at a high volume. This leads to an increase in demand. As demand increases, the available supply also decreases.

What does market demand depend on?

Market factors affecting demand of consumer goods. The demand for a good increases or decreases depending on several factors. This includes the product's price, perceived quality, advertising spend, consumer income, consumer confidence, and changes in taste and fashion.

Who controls the demand in supply and demand?

Supply and demand are in turn determined by technology and the conditions under which people operate. At one extreme, the market could be populated by a large number of virtually identical sellers and buyers (for example, the market for ballpoint pens).

What are the two laws of demand and supply?

The law of demand holds that the demand level for a product or a resource will decline as its price rises, and rise as the price drops. Conversely, the law of supply says higher prices boost supply of an economic good while lower ones tend to diminish it.

What factors affect demand and supply?

Price fluctuations are a strong factor affecting supply and demand. When a product gets expensive enough that the average consumer no longer feels it is worth it to buy the product, then the demand declines. This leads to cuts in production that will hopefully stabilize the product's value.

What factors affect demand and demand?

Demand may be defined as the quantity of a commodity that a consumer is able and willing to buy, at each possible price, over a given period of time. • Essential elements of demand are quantity, ability, willingness, prices, and period of time.

Which factors affect supply?

Generally, the supply of a product depends on its price and other variables such as the cost of production.

a. Price. Price can be understood as what the consumer is willing to pay to receive a good or service. ...

b. Cost of production. ...

c. Technology. ...

d. Governments' policies. ...

e. Transportation condition.

How does supply and demand work together?

It's a fundamental economic principle that when supply exceeds demand for a good or service, prices fall. When demand exceeds supply, prices tend to rise. There is an inverse relationship between the supply and prices of goods and services when demand is unchanged.

What happens to supply when demand increases?

An increase in demand, all other things unchanged, will cause the equilibrium price to rise; quantity supplied will increase. A decrease in demand will cause the equilibrium price to fall; quantity supplied will decrease.

What is the theory of demand?

Demand theory describes the way that changes in the quantity of a good or service demanded by consumers affects its price in the market, The theory states that the higher the price of a product is, all else equal, the less of it will be demanded, inferring a downward sloping demand curve.

What are the 4 basic laws of supply and demand?

1) If the supply increases and demand stays the same, the price will go down. 2) If the supply decreases and demand stays the same, the price will go up. 3) If the supply stays the same and demand increases, the price will go up. 4) If the supply stays the same and demand decreases, the price will go down.

The different types of demand are as follows:

i. Individual and Market Demand: ...

ii. Organization and Industry Demand: ...

iii. Autonomous and Derived Demand: ...

iv. Demand for Perishable and Durable Goods: ...

v. Short-term and Long-term Demand:

What creates demand for a product?

You can create demand for a unique product if you can manage to solve a persistent problem for the consumer. People are always running away from pain, and providing them with an outlet is a sure-fire way to create massive demand for your goods.

What are the 7 factors that affect supply?

The seven factors which affect the changes of supply are as follows: (i) Natural Conditions (ii) Technical Progress (iii) Change in Factor Prices (iv) Transport Improvements (v) Calamities (vi) Monopolies (vii) Fiscal Policy.

What can affect demand?

Factors Affecting Demand

Price of the Product. ...

The Consumer's Income. ...

The Price of Related Goods. ...
The Tastes and Preferences of Consumers. ...
The Consumer's Expectations. ...
The Number of Consumers in the Market.
What are the three factors affecting demand?
The demand for a product will be influenced by several factors:

Price. Usually viewed as the most important factor that affects demand. ...

Income levels. ...
Consumer tastes and preferences. ...
Competition. ...
Fashions.
What are the 4 factors of supply?
The four factors that can shift the supply curve include natural conditions, input prices, technology, and government.
What causes increase in supply?
If the cost of production is lower, the profits available at a given price will increase, and producers will produce more. With more produced at every price, the supply curve will shift to the right, meaning an increase in supply.
What causes supply changes?
A change in supply is an economic term that describes when the suppliers of a given good or service alter production or output. A change in supply can occur as a result of new technologies, such as more efficient or less expensive production processes, or a change in the number of competitors in the market.
Is supply and demand a good strategy?

When it comes to profit placement, supply and demand zones can be a great tool as well. Always place your profit target ahead of a zone so that you don't risk giving back all your profits when the open interest in that zone is filled.

How is demand created?
Demand creation is a process that fuels the revenue pipeline so the sales team can meet or exceed their quotas. In other words, it takes your big idea — the creative appeal of your brand — and turns it into sales. That sounds a lot like demand generation, which often gets confused with lead generation.
What are the two parts of demand?
Economists define demand as the quantity of a good or service that buyers are willing and able to buy at all possible prices during a certain time period.

Notice that there are two components to demand: willingness to purchase and ability to pay.

Can we control demand?

If you're willing to think and act strategically, you can easily manipulate the laws of supply and demand. It should be surprising to learn, however, that by manipulating the laws of supply and demand, you can make more profit in less time and with far fewer headaches

How do you control demand?

Here are five short-term actions to improve your demand variability management plans in this time of uncertainty:

Maintain transparent, proactive relationships with your suppliers. ...

Activate alternate sources of supply. ...

Reduce lead times. ...

Update inventory policy and planning. ...

Align supply and demand management.

What are the 8 types of demand?

There are 8 states of demand: negative demand, no demand, latent demand, falling demand, irregular demand, full demand, overfull demand and unwholesome demand.

What is Demand?

Types of Determinants of Demand. Every factor has a unique impact on demand. ...

Price of the Product. ...

The Income of the Consumers. ...

Number of Buyers in the Market. ...

Consumer's Expectations. ...

Tastes and Preferences of The Consumers. ...

Complement Goods. ...

Substitute Product.

What is theory of supply?

The law of supply is a fundamental principle of economic theory which states that, keeping other factors constant, an increase in price results in an increase in quantity supplied. In other words, there is a direct relationship between price and quantity: quantities respond in the same direction as price changes.

What are the types of supply?

There are five types of supply—market supply, short-term supply, long-term supply, joint supply, and composite supply.

Which comes first supply or demand?
Demand comes first and it's followed by the corresponding supplies. Supply and demand are both very important to economic activity. Supply is the total amount of a particular good or service available at a given time to consumers at a given price. Demand is a representation of a consumer's desire to purchase goods and services; it acts as a measurement of a consumer's willingness to purchase a specific good or service at a given price. These two economic forces influence each other; they are both important for the economy because they impact the prices of consumer goods and services within an economy and the quantities produced and consumed. Supply and demand are both keys to understanding the economy because they reflect the prices and quantities of consumer goods and services within an economy.

What are the relationship between demand and supply?
According to market economy theory, the relationship between supply and demand balances out at a point in the future; this point is called the equilibrium price.
Economists and companies analyze the relationship between supply and demand when making strategic product decisions. Both economists and companies analyze the relationship between supply and demand when making strategic product decisions. The assumption behind a market economy is that supply and demand are the best determinants for an economy's growth and health.
Consumer Behavior Influences Demand
One way that companies or economists might analyze this relationship is to create graphs that chart the equilibrium price of certain goods and services in order to determine product development and their production schedule. Consumer behavior dictates which products are produced and sold because consumers create the demand that companies attempt to meet. As a result, companies may study consumer behavior in an attempt to understand the current demand and predict future demand. It is vital that companies maintain the capacity to produce enough of a good or service that they can satisfy consumer demands.
Supply and demand are two sides of the same market coin. Generally, supply is how much of something is available or will be produced at a certain price. Demand is how much of something people want to purchase or consume at a certain price. One way to develop a more precise

relationship between the two is to consider how the price of something affects its supply and its demand. Generally when the price of a good goes up, so does the supply, since firms are willing to create more when they can sell at higher prices. But when the price of a good goes up consumers will, at the same time, generally demand less. It is the interaction of supply and demand that determines how much will be produced and consumed and at what price, converging to a state known as equilibrium.

CHAPTER TWO

Human social job change demand and supply relationship

The relationship between social change and human behavior

Human Behavioral network job brings social economic benefits

Whether human social job change it depends on social job demand more or job supply more? What does human network job mean ? Why may human network job be popular? Why human network job behavior may influence economy ?

Nowadays internet is popular to use. We can apply internet to find data , search any new things, even earn money. Why does internet may become huma network job source. For example, e-publish may be one kind of new human network job. Any authors may apply internet channel to help them to sell electronic or paper books from e-publisher web store. They may apply facebook, you tub etc. any online channel to promote themselves new books to let new readers to know whether when they may buy themselves favourable new topic books to read from electronic publisher web store.

Thus, future electronic publisher industry may help any authors to build internet network platform to help them to sell and promote ot advertise their any one new electronic or paper book topic to let global any one reader to choose to buy their any new topic books from electronic publisher web store easily and conveniently. However, it implies that electronic network platform author may be one kind of future new human network job in our societies.

How electronic network platform author job may bring economy benefit in macro economy view? A person can have few friends, contacts and still be very influential if these few
friends and contacts are themselves highly influential, e.g. one author must not need to know any one reader in global society. When they like to choose any electronic books from electronic internet network platform. They may become the author's any one topic book buyer, when they feel the author's any one topic book is fun and attract they make decision to buth the strange author whose the topic book from electronic book publisher's platform web store conventiently in short time. Although, they are strangers, they do not know themselves , but the reader can understand what it way that made Google from writing platofrm to create new creative mind and typing network job method to replace traditional hand writing book method for global authors. It will be one kind of new human network writing job.

Hence, global any one reader can apply an innovative search engine , such as google.com to find whether whom author personal new topic books are value to read from internet.
Then, the electroniuc publisher's web store may be new book store platform sale network to help the author to sell many electronic or paper books from electronic network platform
in short time. So, internet may be future new network plaform to help global any one author to create network writing job absolutely. Furthermore, internet may be popular social media
to help any one author to build goold relationship between his/her readers. It is one kind of new network, human network job. New authors do not need to buy many paper books to prepare to put in any one book shop warehouse. Their every book can print on demand to reduce out of book stock in any one book shop. They may choose to sell either electronic books or paper books both from any one book publisher web store. So, electronic network platform may be one kind of good writing channel to help human authors to create income and it can also help authors to bring new creative mind and new topic fun content books to let readers to know and buy to read from electronic publisher network platform.

Why does human behavior may be one kind of new human network job to bring global economic advantages. ALthough, it may be free income or without inocme, but the person does the network behavior, his/her behavior may be bring advantages to influence many other people's health.

For this case, when a worker in a coffee shop in an airport gets a vaccination aganinst the flu, it does not only helps him or her stay healthy, but also helps the many travellers who might otherwise have been inflected if that workers caught the flu. So, the externality , the result implies the vaccination of even a part of a community conveys benefits to the whole community. For example, governments pay special attention to the vaccinations of school children, teachers, health mothers, and the elderly, categories of people particularly susceptible not only to catching, but also to transmitting a disease.

It is not accidential that governments are heavily involved with vaccination . When there are externalities, free market, fail to persuade individual incentives with society's

their the worker's decision of whether to get a vaccine ends up attracting whether other people get sick. The workers might not fully take all these other people's potential suffering into account when making her or his vaccination decision.

As Stanford University does many suggestions, understand this and tries to help them make the right decisions and so providers free flu vaccines for its staff and students.

Small pockets of unvaccinated individuals can allow a disease to gain a spread more widely well-being. For example, parent weighing the costs and benefits of a vaccine for their child is not always thinking of the consequences of that vaccination to other people. THese are markets in which subsidizing or regulating behavior can make everyone better off. Because the reason for requiring that a child be vaccinated before enrolling in school is not just to protect that child, because each child's vaccination affects others via potential contagions.

On conclusion, it seems that many traditional paper book publish business begain to change to electronic book publish business. Due, to online technology existence, it influences many readers choose to buy electronic books to read. Hence, due to readers reading demand change which is from paper book reading habit to electonic book reading habit.Then,it explains that electornic book supply number depends on electronic book reader reading demand in economic view.

Robots take our jobs behavioral and economy influences

Robot job behavior brings economy influences

Whether robot labor needs are depended on employer labor demand more or robot labor number supply more? If one day robots can replace human to do simple, even complex jobs. They will bring what influences to our global societial economy.The popular economic refrain declares that the global middle class is dying and robots will soon take our jobs, e.g. shopping center customer service jobs, library service jobs, cinema ticket sale jobs, restaurant kitchen cooker jobs, even, bus drivers, taxi drivers etc. public transport driving jobs, accountant, doctors etc. professional jobs. Whether it is beautiful or petty matter if our future societies have many human jobs can be replaced to do from robots. Businessman must may reduce to employ employees and reduce to pay salary or wage, when robots can be replaced to do their employees tasks. But, societies must bring unemployement rate rises , due to societies will have many people loss jobs when their employers choose to buy robots to serve their clients or do any office tasks or customer service or cleaning etc. tasks.

In micro economy view, employers may save money in long term, but in macro economy view, it will cause unemployment ratio rises , even crime rate rises when there are many people lose jobs in societies. These models of doom, though, fail to account for the hundreds of businesses riding the waves of change in their industries when robots may be invented to replace human to do many simple , even complex tasks in our future societies.

WE may image that one small factory needs to manufacture fishes canes to sell to supermarket, the small , cheaper stuff and higher margin parts of the fishes manufacture industry. Before, this factory needs to employe many human factory workers need to help every fresh customer makeing the perfect fishing gear, designed for performance, durability, and cost in order to achieve to manufacture every fish cane in whole fished processing manufacturing stages. Every worker needs to spend about 15 to twenty minutes to finish every fish cane , till to delivery to any supermarket to sell. If this fish canes manufacturing factory can apply manufacturing robots to help them to finish any one working tasks , every robot can only spend five minutes to finish whole fresh fish cane manufacturing process. Thus, every robot can help this factory save 10 to 15 minutes time to finsh every fish cane manufacturing process. IN fact, time is money, because when every robot can help this factory to reduce 10 to 15 minutes time to compare human

worker. Then, this factory can finish about 20 fish canes in one hour if it can use robot to help it to manufacture fish canes. Otherwise, if this factory still use human workers to help it to manufacture fish canes, then it can finsh about 3 to 4 fish canes in one hour. SO, the manufacturing efficiency ensures that robots must help this fish manufacturing factory to raise fish canes number more than human workers. So, in robotic behavioral economy view, manufacturing robots must help this fish canes manufacturing factory to raise fish canes manufacturing number and deliver increasing number to supermarkets to prepare to sell every day. Robots can help this fish canes manufacturing factory bring manufacturing time saving, rising manufacturing efficiency, improving performance and reducing wages expenditure long time advantages in micro economy view. However, manufacturing robots can also bring disadvanages to society, e.g. increasing unemployment ratio, increasing crime rate,
this factory workers will lose jobs and income, they need earn social welfare from government and increasing government finance pressure in short time, even long time in macro economic view.

Stanford University graduate program in economics, Scott lecturer explained that "in demand and supply economic theory for robots supply and demand case, robots supply number increasing may influence human workers demand number decrease. It sometimes calls " the efficient frontier".
No specific human beings were mentioned in any of economics classes. As robots supply and demand in market case, They (robots) may be purely theoretical " agents" who reached to the most reasonable sale prices in order to persuade any one businessman buyer to make manufacturing robot buying decision whether robots can help him / her to bring how much saving time , saving money, saving cost, improving performance, efficiency economic benefit before he/she plans to reduce workers number when he/ she decides to apply robots to replace human workers in his/her factory or office or any service department, e.g. cinema ticket sale service, shopping center customer service, shopping center cleaning , supermarket customer service etc. service or sale tasks. When robots can replace human to do any one of these tasks in any organizations. So, robots may be human worker agents who reached to prices the way robots would react to a software
command. There was nothing that explained why some people thrived and others did n't or why truly brilliant, hardworking people could fail when much lazier folks succeeded." Having been admitted to the Stanford

University graduate program in economics, Scott lecturer hoped to get his answers there.

How robots influence our future social changing? Using the right technology can be a boon to your business in this economy. For internet example, it is easier than ever to find well-matched customers all around the world, to stay in contact with them, and to more quickly design the products they want. If you focus solely on being cutting -edge, though you risk letting the technology
take over what should be very robust relationships with your customers , employees, and colleagues. IN nowaddays society, technoligical advances and cutomation, personal
relationships in business are more crucial than ever. I mean that robots can not replace human to serve clients to let them to feel more comfortable and passion more easily. For shoe shop case example, if the shoe shop apply one robot to serve its clients to replace human shoe salesperson to serve its shoe customers. Robots ensure that they can not persuade every shoe potential buyer to make shoe buying decision more easily when robots need to contact every shoe potential buyer. The reason is simple, because robots can not touch any one shoe buyer individual emotion very easier.
If the shoe buyer needs the robots to help him/her to choose any right shoe styles when he/she can not feel himself / herself can make the most right shoe style choice decision. The robots can not replace human shoe salesperson to make shoe style choice judgement more easily. They must need longer time to analyze whether which shoe style may be the most suitable to the shoe buyer. Otherwise, human shoe salesperson may attempt to make the most right shoe style choice decision to help any one shoe buyer to chooce the most right style shoe because he/she owns shoe style sale experience, shoe style knowledge, the most important reason is that they can feel every shoe customer individual emotion to touch whether he/she will feel comfortable or happy when they attempt to help every shoe customer to seek the most right shoe style in every shoe customer whole shoe searching processing. Othwerwise, serving robots are only one machine, they can not touch or feel every shoe customer individual emotion whether he/she feel comfortable or unhappy or happy when they need to contact them in whole shoe searching processing. Hence, I believe that some tasks robots can
not repalce human staff to do very easily. Otherwise, robots may bring disadvanatges to let any one businessman to loss his/her customers, due to

robots can not touch every customer
emotion to compare human staff in service tasks more easily. Robots serving customer behaviors may cause money lose and customers number lose to the shop in micro economic view.

On conclusion, in demand and supply economic theory for robots supply and demand case, robots supply number increasing may influence human workers demand number decrease. So, it seems that robots number supply will be depended on global robots supply number more than robots demand number because when human began to accept robots to replace human to do general simple jobs in global labor market. Then, it means that global robots labor number must need to be increased in order to satisfy global businessmen workers number need. If any kinds of robot workers manufacture number is not enough to be supplied to let global future businessmen to buy, then robot supply will be shortage and they can not provide to satisfy global businessmen robots labour purchase need. So, future robot number will be depended on supply more than demand.

Chapter 3 Human intellectual demand and supply behavior relationship

Intellectual human economic behaviors

What does intellectual human economic behaviors mean ? Human foolish behavior is depended on social enjoyment need more or material social supply more? I believe that when we choose or decide to do intellectual behaviors, then our societies will be influenced to bring economic growth in consequence.I shall attempt to indicate pollution case to explain how and why eithet our intellectual or foolish behaviors may bring economic growth or recession in consequence as below:
On one hand, for air pollution social case aspect example, if we only consider to buy cars to drive for working aim or holiday leisure aim. Then, our societies air will be polluted. Our health will be influenced to bad. Our car driving behaviors may cause global environment air pollution serously. In long tiem, global air pollution will bring our bodies health to be bad. Although, ourselves car driving behaviors may bring our driving travelling leisure enjoyment and comfortable feeling in short time, also we so not need to pay public transport fare often, but we need to compensate ourselves health economic intangible loss due to air pollution , when cars number increases, dirty air will cause ouselves health to become bad.
In the result, we will need to pay more medical expenditure when we are

old age, due to ourselves bodies will become bad, due to we breathe global dirty air every day, due to ourselves cars pollute air in long time, e.g. 10 to 20 years, even 30 more without limited air pollution environment. So, driving cars behavior may be one kind of human foolish behavior and our foolish behavior may bring ourselves future long time medical expenditure absolutely.

One the other hand, water pollution social aspect, if we often keep much rubblish to pollute sea, oil exploration porcessing pollute ocean , ships gas pollute ocaen, then fishes will eat polluted food and drive dirty water, due to global ocean is polluted.

In fact, because human only to conside how to buy boats to carry on leisure enjoyment activities, or catch cruises to travel on the sea. Also, oil manufacturers only consider researching anywhere to find new oil exploration places to manufacture oil product, when their oil exploration processes pollute ocarn . Consequently, global fishes drink polluted warer or eat polluted food. They will have poison. SO, human will have high chance to eat poison polluted fishes, due to fishes are poison or are polluted. So, human is doing foolish activities, we only hope to find oil exploration places to pollute ocean or we only spend money to buy ticket to catch ships to travel anywhere in global ocean. All of these human foolish behaviors will bring pollution to global ocean. On consequently, we will need to compensate to eat polluted or dirty or poision fishes, ourselves bodies health will be bad. In long time, we need have high chance to pay medical expenditure when we are old. So, pollution case may be one good example to explain how and why human foolish behavior may influence ourselves future need to compensate serious medical loss.

All of these human foolish behavior will bring pollution to global ocean. On consequently, we will need to compensate to eat polluted or dirty or poison fished , ourselves bodies health will be bad. In long time, we will have high chance to pay medical expenditure, when we are old. So, pollution case may be one good example to explain how and why human ourselves intellectual or foolish behaviors may influence future long time economic loss or economic growth or recession in micro and micro economic view.

On another water pollution aspect hand, if we often keep rubbish to sea, oil exploration processing pollutes ocean and ships' gas pollute ocean, then fishes will eat polluted food and drink dirty water, due to fishes will eat polluted food and drink dirty sea water because the global ocean is polluted seriously.

In fact, because human only consider how to buy boats to carry on any leisure water activities, or catches cruises to travel on the sea. Also, oil manufacturers only consider any where to find oil exploratin places to manufacture oil products from ocean, when their pol exploration processes can plooute ocean. Consequently, global fishes drink polluted water or eat direty food. They will have poison. So, human will have high chance to eat poison fishes.

Otherwise, such as pollutin case, it can infuence inflation or deflation. Consequently, the reason indicates supply and demand theory. If air pollution is serious, then we will consider health issue, global cars demand number may be influenced to reduce, when global cars number demand will reduce, global car prices and supply number will need to change to fall down in order to attract or persuade global car consumers choose to make car purchase decision.

Hence, global car manufacture number and car price will be influenced to reduce, due to global air pollution issue. Consequently, deflation will occur because when the country citizen usually does not spend much extra saving money to buy car expensive goods. Money value will be low. Otherwise, if global cair pollution is not serious, human considers to buy cars to enjoy driving leisure lives. So, global car demand is influenced to increase , also global car price will also influenced to increase.

Consequently, gobal human will choose to buy cars to drive. Due to we accept to spend extra saving to buy expensive car goods. Car sale price and supply may be influenced to rise up. Money value is influenced to reduce. Inflation may be influenced, due to global car consumers number increases, we would not have extra money to spend easily. Car expensive goods expenditure influences our spending habit to avoid to make car purchase decision more easily. So, human intellectual or foolish activities may bring inflation or deflation consequency in possible indirectly in macro economic view.

On conclusion, above pollution case explain that how and why human intellectual or foolish economic behaviors may bring inflation or deflation consequency as wll as economic growth or recession consequency as well as any goods demand and supply increasing or decreasing consequency. It implies that human behavior may have indirect relationship to influence any goods demand and supply number to either increase or decrease result as well as any goods price will be influenced to increase or decrease in micro and macro economic view. Hence, Human foolish behavior is depended on social enjoyment need more or material social supply more because human needs to raise enjoyment feel , so we will choose to do foolish behavior, e.g. air pollution, when many people choose to buy cars to drive to replace catch public transport. So, such as car market, it depends on car demand number more than car supply number absolutely in demand and supply view.

The relationship between social change and human behavior

Why does economic changes may influence human individual behavioral change? I shall attempt to indicate shopping behavior and staying at home behavior to explain their case and effect relationsip as below:
Human behavior can be influenced by economic change or economic change can be influenced by human behavior? Why does recession may influence consumers reduce shopping desire? In social recession suitation, it is possible that many people lose jobs suddenly, due to businessmen lose many customers. They need to make decision to reduce employees number in order to continue to keep businesses. Consequently, many firms (organizations) their employees may lose jobs. When they have much time, due to lose jobs, they will feel to avoid to spend too much time and money to go to shopping often. Many losing jobs people, they will often stay at homes. So, they will reduce time to go to shopping, then non essential products won't their preferable choice purchase products. Hence, recession will change many losing jobs people their shopping or consumption desires to avoid to buy non essential products often . Usually when economic boom, many people have jobs to do because consumers number must increase when many people have jobs to do. Then, many people can accept to spend money to buy non essential products often. Many people feel spend time to go to shopping can satisfy their purchase of any kinds of new products useful psychology or desire. So, recession is one good example to explain it can influence many people do not like often to leave homes to go to shopping easily. Many people like to stay at homes, becaue they feel worry about spending too much shopping time when they leave homes. Their staying home time is one good negative shopping behavior example. So, economic change may influence human individual behavior changes , they have direct cause and efect relationship in behavioral economic view.
May human behavior influence economic change? Is it possible that human behavior may bring the country social economic change in macro economic or micro behavioral economic view ? I shall indicate publishing industry example. Do you feel that if there are many students feel learning is very important when they read many books or many of students feel interesting

to read or they have reading new books in habit, then it is possible that the country will have many students like to spend time to go to any book shops to choose the books, they feel that they can help they learn new knowledge. Then the country will increase students number, they often spend time to visit any one book shop every week. Their visiting book shops behavior which may become their habits. So, the country will increase students number, they often spend time to visit book shops. Also, it implies that visiting book shops behaviors may be their behavioral habits.

So, when the country has many students often spend time to visit book shops , their visiting book shops behaviors may help any one book shop to raise books sale chance. So, the country's student individual often visiting book shop behaviors, their habitual visiting book shops behaviors must may assist help any one book shop to increase books sale number absolutely.

Consequently, any one book shop , its books sale bumber must be influenced to increase to increase because the country will have many students like or feel need visit book shops habit in order to choose any suitable books to buy to read at home in order to raise themselves learning effort. When the country has many bok shops often have many students visit their book shops, then their books sale number may be influenced to increase. It explain why student individual visiting book shop behavior may help any one book shop sale number increases also. So, visiting shops products sale number is depended on online products supply number, if online products supply number increases, then it may cause many customers choose to buy the kind of products from online webstore. So, any shop products sale number will depend on onlint products supply number in supply and demand view.

CHAPTER THREE

Human intellectual demand and supply behavior relationship

Intellectual human economic behaviors

What does intellectual human economic behaviors mean ? Human foolish behavior is depended on social enjoyment need more or material social supply more? I believe that when we choose or decide to do intellectual behaviors, then our societies will be influenced to bring economic growth in consequence.I shall attempt to indicate pollution case to explain how and why eithet our intellectual or foolish behaviors may bring economic growth or recession in consequence as below:

On one hand, for air pollution social case aspect example, if we only consider to buy cars to drive for working aim or holiday leisure aim. Then, our societies air will be polluted. Our health will be influenced to bad. Our car driving behaviors may cause global environment air pollution serously. In long tiem, global air pollution will bring our bodies health to be bad. Although, ourselves car driving behaviors may bring our driving travelling leisure enjoyment and comfortable feeling in short time, also we so not need to pay public transport fare often, but we need to compensate ourselves health economic intangible loss due to air pollution , when cars number increases, dirty air will cause ouselves health to become bad.

In the result, we will need to pay more medical expenditure when we are old age, due to ourselves bodies will become bad, due to we breathe global dirty air every day, due to ourselves cars pollute air in long time, e.g. 10 to 20 years, even 30 more without limited air pollution environment. So, driving cars behavior may be one kind of human foolish behavior and our foolish behavior may bring ourselves future long time medical expenditure absolutely.

One the other hand, water pollution social aspect, if we often keep much rubblish to pollute sea, oil exploration porcessing pollute ocean , ships gas pollute ocaen, then fishes will eat polluted food and drive dirty water, due to global ocean is polluted.

In fact, because human only to conside how to buy boats to carry on leisure enjoyment activities, or catch cruises to travel on the sea. Also, oil manufacturers only consider researching anywhere to find new oil exploration places to manufacture oil product, when their oil exploration processes pollute ocarn . Consequently, global fishes drink polluted warer or eat polluted food. They will have poison. SO, human will have high chance to eat poison polluted fishes, due to fishes are poison or are polluted. So, human is doing foolish activities, we only hope to find oil exploration places to pollute ocean or we only spend money to buy ticket to catch ships to travel anywhere in global ocean. All of these human foolish behaviors will bring pollution to global ocean. On consequently, we will need to compensate to eat polluted or dirty or poision fishes, ourselves bodies health will be bad. In long time, we need have high chance to pay medical expenditure when we are old. So, pollution case may be one good example to explain how and why human foolish behavior may influence ourselves future need to compensate serious medical loss.

All of these human foolish behavior will bring pollution to global ocean. On consequently, we will need to compensate to eat polluted or dirty or poison fished , ourselves bodies health will be bad. In long time, we will have high chance to pay medical expenditure, when we are old. So, pollution case may be one good example to explain how and why human ourselves intellectual or foolish behaviors may influence future long time economic loss or economic growth or recession in micro and micro economic view.

On another water pollution aspect hand, if we often keep rubbish to sea, oil exploration processing pollutes ocean and ships' gas pollute ocean, then fishes will eat polluted food and drink dirty water, due to fishes will eat polluted food and drink dirty sea water because the global ocean is polluted seriously.

In fact, because human only consider how to buy boats to carry on any leisure water activities, or catches cruises to travel on the sea. Also, oil manufacturers only consider any where to find oil exploratin places to manufacture oil products from ocean, when their pol exploration processes can plooute ocean. Consequently, global fishes drink polluted water or eat direty food. They will have poison. So, human will have high chance to eat poison fishes.

Otherwise, such as pollutin case, it can infuence inflation or deflation. Consequently, the reason indicates supply and demand theory. If air pollution is serious, then we will consider health issue, global cars demand number may be influenced to reduce, when global cars number demand will reduce, global car prices and supply number will need to change to fall down in order to attract or persuade global car consumers choose to make car purchase decision.

Hence, global car manufacture number and car price will be influenced to reduce, due to global air pollution issue. Consequently, deflation will occur because when the country citizen usually does not spend much extra saving money to buy car expensive goods. Money value will be low. Otherwise, if global cair pollution is not serious, human considers to buy cars to enjoy driving leisure lives. So, global car demand is influenced to increase , also global car price will also influenced to increase.

Consequently, gobal human will choose to buy cars to drive. Due to we accept to spend extra saving to buy expensive car goods. Car sale price and supply may be influenced to rise up. Money value is influenced to reduce. Inflation may be influenced, due to global car consumers number increases, we would not have extra money to spend easily. Car expensive goods expenditure influences our spending habit to avoid to make car purchase decision more easily. So, human intellectual or foolish activities may bring inflation or deflation consequency in possible indirectly in macro economic view.

On conclusion, above pollution case explain that how and why human intellectual or foolish economic behaviors may bring inflation or deflation consequency as wll as economic growth or recession consequency as well as any goods demand and supply increasing or decreasing consequency. It implies that human behavior may have indirect relationship to influence any goods demand and supply number to either increase or decrease result as well as any goods price will be influenced to increase or decrease in micro and macro economic view. Hence, Human foolish behavior is depended on social enjoyment need more or material social supply more because human needs to raise enjoyment feel , so we will choose to do foolish behavior, e.g. air pollution, when many people choose to buy cars to drive to replace catch public transport. So, such as car market, it depends on car demand number more than car supply number absolutely in demand and supply view.

The relationship between social change and human behavior

Why does economic changes may influence human individual behavioral change? I shall attempt to indicate shopping behavior and staying at home behavior to explain their case and effect relationsip as below:
Human behavior can be influenced by economic change or economic change can be influenced by human behavior? Why does recession may influence consumers reduce shopping desire? In social recession suitation, it is possible that many people lose jobs suddenly, due to businessmen lose many customers. They need to make decision to reduce employees number in order to continue to keep businesses. Consequently, many firms (organizations) their employees may lose jobs. When they have much time, due to lose jobs, they will feel to avoid to spend too much time and money to go to shopping often. Many losing jobs people, they will often stay at homes. So, they will reduce time to go to shopping, then non essential products won't their preferable choice purchase products. Hence, recession will change many losing jobs people their shopping or consumption desires to avoid to buy non essential products often . Usually when economic boom, many people have jobs to do because consumers number must increase when many people have jobs to do. Then, many people can accept to spend money to buy non essential products often. Many people feel spend time to go to shopping can satisfy their purchase of any kinds of new products useful psychology or desire. So, recession is one good example to explain it can influence many people do not like often to leave homes to go to shopping easily. Many people like to stay at homes, becaue they feel worry about spending too much shopping time when they leave homes. Their staying home time is one good negative shopping behavior example. So, economic change may influence human individual behavior changes , they have direct cause and efect relationship in behavioral economic view.
May human behavior influence economic change? Is it possible that human behavior may bring the country social economic change in macro economic or micro behavioral economic view ? I shall indicate publishing industry example. Do you feel that if there are many students feel learning is very important when they read many books or many of students feel interesting to read or they have reading new books in habit, then it is possible that the country will have many students like to spend time to go to any book shops to choose the books, they feel that they can help they learn new knowledge.

Then the country will increase students number, they often spend time to visit any one book shop every week. Their visiting book shops behavior which may become their habits. So, the country will increase students number, they often spend time to visit book shops. Also, it implies that visiting book shops behaviors may be their behavioral habits.

So, when the country has many students often spend time to visit book shops , their visiting book shops behaviors may help any one book shop to raise books sale chance. So, the country's student individual often visiting book shop behaviors, their habitual visiting book shops behaviors must may assist help any one book shop to increase books sale number absolutely.

Consequently, any one book shop , its books sale bumber must be influenced to increase to increase because the country will have many students like or feel need visit book shops habit in order to choose any suitable books to buy to read at home in order to raise themselves learning effort. When the country has many bok shops often have many students visit their book shops, then their books sale number may be influenced to increase. It explain why student individual visiting book shop behavior may help any one book shop sale number increases also. So, visiting shops products sale number is depended on online products supply number, if online products supply number increases, then it may cause many customers choose to buy the kind of products from online webstore. So, any shop products sale number will depend on onlint products supply number in supply and demand view.

CHAPTER FOUR

Human social demand and supply relationship

How human productive behavior may influence economic development

May any country which citizen behavior assist themselves country development? It is one cause and effect economic question. I mean that if the country itself citicen can not concentrate mind or energy to choose to do one kind of industry in order to let themselves country can bring the most benefit, then whether the counry itself economy can bring the most serious economic benefit. I shall attempt to indicate these countries themselves indistry choice to explain whether these countries themselves citizen productive behavior may help themselves countries to achieve the largest economic benefits. I shall indicate as below:

New Zealand farmer individual wine productive behavior

For New Zealand country example, this country concerns itself effort is foucs on farming agricultural aspect. So, this country has many farmers concentrate on farming agricultural aspect. May New Zealanders choose to spend time to produce different kinds of wines, e.g. wine or red grape wine is for the people are eating meat, or they are eating dinner.

When these New Zealanders their behaviors choose to do farming or agriculture to grow and produce different kinds of taste of white or red grape wine drinking products job. Themselves grape agriculture behavior will influence these New Zealanders themselves, they can learn how to improve different kinds of grape wine drinking products in order to achieve every kinds of white or read grape wines taste improving aim during their white or red grape producing process.

Why can New Zealander every individual white or read grape wine producers improve their white or read grape wine taste more easily? In behavioral economic view, it can explain that why any one New Zealander white or read grape wine producer can be encouraged or excited or persuaded to concentrate nervous and energy and effort to learn how to improve their white or red grape wine products easily.

In fact, New Zealand is one agricultural food export country. It has good natural environment resource , e.g. land, seed to provide any one farmer to produce themselves any kinds of agricultrual food products, e.g. fruit, or wine food products. Because New Zealanders know themselves country has enough natural resource . So, in common, many New Zealanders choose to attempt to do farming agricultural jobs in order to export themselves any kinds of fruit or meat or wine products to overseas or sell to domestic in order to earn profit.

So, when these New Zealand farmers number has been increasing every year. This country farmers will feel themsleves competition between this New Zealand farmers themselves are serious due to they may feel New Zealanders choose to do agriculture businesses in order to export themselves different kinds of farming food to overseas or sell to local to earn profit.

Hence, when many New Zealand farmers feel that farmers number has been increasing every year. They will feel themselves competition is serious. They must need to spend much time and nervous and effort to research what method is the best how to produce the best taste of white or red grape wine products in order to let local or overseas wine buyers to choose to buy his/her producing white or read grpae products to drink.

Hence, in competition psychological view, may influence many New Zealand white or reaad wine producers had been beginning to change their learning behavior on researching what method is the best in order to produce the best quality of taste red or white wine products to sell in order to attract overseas or local white or read grape wine drinkers to choose to buy his/her wine products. Their behavior will focus on learning how to raising or improving white or read grape wine taste method more than only focus on producing a large number white or red grape wine products. They believe wine quality is more important to compare wine producing number. So, New Zealand wine producers themselves wine producers behaviors have been changing on concentrating on researching wine quality method aspect more then wine producing number aspect in behavioral economic view.

America high technological productive behavior

For America example, US is one high technological country, it owns many high technological knowledge talent inventors, e.g. computer science inventors. Hence, US must attract many diferent countries owning high technological computer inventors choose to go to US to develop their computer science profession career. Also, it seems that when many computer science inventors or professions choose to go to US to develop themselves computer science new career. In behavioral economic view, due to their leaving themselves countries choice, which may bring influence themselve country job behaviors need to be changed. They must need to adapt US new live. Because they will forgive their past computer science job. These computer science professionals need to spend time to adapt US new lives. They " past computer science job behaviors" will need to be changed to their new US any computer employer's new computer science job model.

Because their traditional computer science jobs needed to be forgot in their themselves countries. They will feel their old computer science job knowledge and behavior needed to change in order to let their US any one new of computer company employer feels satisfactory to accept their new working behavior in any one US computer organization.

So, on the other hand, many US computer company employer will feel that they must need time to accept any one new overseas computer science professions their working behaviors, their working attitude daily, because these foreign comouter science professional, their past computer working behaviors and working attitude must be different to US domestic computer science professions.

In behavioral economic view, these overseas computer science professions, their working behaviors and attitude must be needed to change in order to adapt any one US new computer company itself domestic or local computer science professional stafs themselves daily working behaviors and attitude because these overseas and local computer science professionals must need to team work together.

In behavioral economic view, it is only one way that foreign computer science professionals must need to change themselves past country traditiona daily working behaviors and attitude in order to cooperate with these US local computer science professionals in teams more easily.

Consequently, if these foreign compute science professionals can change their past working behaviors and attitude to let any one US local computer science professional feels to cooperate with them easily in short time. Then, the US computer company itself whole computer professional teams themselves efficiencies will be influenced to raised or improved by the changing past working attitude and working behaviors of these foreign computer science professionals. So, in behavioral economic view, only if US any one computer company hopes itself computer teams themselves efficiency can be raised or improved when it decides to employ foreign computer science professionals and US domestic computer science professionals. They need to work in teams together. They must need to let these foreign computer science professionals to know how to change their working behaviors and attitude to let their domestic computer science professionals feel easy to work together. Then, the US computer company itself whole team efficiency must be rasied or improved easily in short time.

- China share market investing behavior

For China share market example, economic development depends on financial market. Because if many Chinese have interest to invest to carry on shares buying and selling activities in orde to learn how to earn shares interest and share profit when the China shareholder can make decision to sell himself/herself shares in the the high price, then he/she can earn money when he/she can sell the China company's shares in the high sale share price position.

If China has many Chinese like to spend time to carry on investing shares activities. Themselves shares buying and selling behaviors will influence China has many companies can increase fund from many Chinese shareholders in order to have enough money to expand or develop themselves businesses in China in long term.

Consequently, when China can have many Chinese like to attempt to carry on buying and selling shares investing behaviors in China share market. Themselves buying and selling shares behaviors can help many Chinese companies have effort to increase enough money or capital in order to continue to do their businesses in long term absolutely. So, it explains why when many Chinese become shareholders , they can assist China will have many companies continue to develop their businesses if many Chinese like to carry on shares buying and selling investing behaviors in long time in China financial investment market nowadays in behavioral economic view.

Why has any individual country have many people invest share behavior which can influence the country's macro consumption desire?
I shall apply shares market buying and selling investment behavior to explaiin why shares investment behavior which may impact the country's overal consumption desire as below:
In behavioral economic view, I assume that when the coutry has many people have interest to attempt to carry on shares buying and selling investment behavior, then their frequent shares buying and selling behaviors which may bring negactive consumption desire or shopping desire of these shares investors their consumer behavior.
The reason is simple, when the country has many share buyers number suddenly been increasing rapidly. Consequently, these large group share investors must need to spend much time to research any kinds of company shares variations, whether when their share prices will rise up of fall down in order to achieve buying the company's shares in the lowest price and selling the company's shares in the highest price level in order to earn profit.
Basic on this reason, they must need to spend much extra time to research share prices changing behavior every day, e.g. one working person will wait to leave his/her job, after he/she can spend time to gather data to research the day's share price changing behavior after dinner. So, the working person's right time may be his/her share price market research behavior. Before he/she may spend his/her night time to go to shopping after dinner, but nowadays, he/she will fogive to do his/her shopping behavior before dinner or after dinner at hight sometime. He/she will make decision to spend much night time to turn on computer to click on share market website to research his/her share purchase choice to investigate whether his/her share price whether it rises up or falls down at the moment in order to make his/her share buying or selling decision at ever night time.
I mean the when the country has many people are share investors, their shares investment behavioral spenging time which will influence many shops lose customers at might often because the country will have many people feel need to spend night time to turn on computer or watch television to investigate share price variation. So, the country will have many people / share investors choose to stay at home in order to carry on share price variation investigation behavior, they need to listen share market update news from radios or watch the share market update news from computer or TV at home every night. Consequenly, they must reduce

times to leave themselves homes at night. So, their shopping behavior also will be reduced. Because these share investors feel need to spend time to investigate share price variation news at homes which can bring economic benefits (high opportunity benefits) when they choose to forgive to leave homes to go to shopping times (opportunity cost) every night.

On conclusion, it seems that when the country has many people are share investors, then their share price investigating behavior may bring negative shopping emotion at night. Consequently, the country's any one shop may lose many customers from this share investor consumer group in behavioral economic view. Hence, when the country's share investors number had been increasing rapidly, it will influence any shops lose many customers from this share investing customer group at night frequenly in short time, even long time in behavioral economic view, because their shopping desires or shopping emotion will be brought negative feeling when they make decisions to spend much time to listen radios or watch TV or computers share price update nes at night. Hence, share market will bring negative impact to influence consumer shopping desire or negative shopping emotion in behavioral economic view.

CHAPTER FIVE

Technology demand and supply relationship

Can technology influence human shopping behavioral change?
Nowadays, technological development has reached mature stage, whether technological mature stage may bring positive or negative shopping emotion influence to global consumers. I shall aplly internet inventin or ecommerce shopping channel tool to explain whether internet technology can bring postive or negative influence to global consumer behavior in behavioral economic view.

Internet is a good technological tool, it brings e-commerce business chance. In fact, commonly, global has have many businessmen choose to use internet channel to carry on their products transactions between global online-buyers and their electronic websites. So, global many shoppers had begun to feel online shopping is more convenient to compare visiting shops shopping. Their shopping behaviors have been changed from internet technological tool. Global has many shoppers choose to buy any products from any overseas or local businessmen their web stores. They only need to spend time to find any businessmen their webstores to choose the most suitable products to pay visa to buy from their webstores. at homes. So, in general, global had have may shoppers had changed their shopping behaviors from visiting shops to visiting webstores at homes often.

So, it seems that internet technological tool had influenced global many shops disappear, but internet webstores will be replaced their actual shops on streets. Some of businessmen either they choose webstores to replace shops or choose websotes and shops both or still keep shops only. Hence, internet tool influences global businessmen have three kinds of products sale channels to let globa local and overseas consumers to choose how to buy their products.

However, in fact, many of global shoppers, youngers and olders had begun to accept to buy any products from webstores. They feel to spend time to leave homes to visit shops , their shopping behaviors will be wasted time to not essential part to their daily lives. Hence, since internet technological invention, it had changed many consumers their traditional visiting shops shopping habit to change to buying products from webstores channel.

However, on the one hand, internet creates webstores ecommerce shopping channel to let global many consumers do not need to leave homes to go to shopping. It brings negative visiting shops shopping emotion to global general consumers nowadays. But on the other hand, it also brings positive visiting internet webstores shopping emotion to global general consumer nowadays. So, it seems that global many consumers feel that they often do not need to spend much time to go out shopping. Many global consumers feel convenient and enjoy to choose any products to buy from different internet webstores, when the online buyer chooses the most suitable product, he she only needs to pay visa card to buy the product from the online seller's webstore conveniently at home.

Hence, online shopping can bring economic benefit to online buyers, e.g. avoiding walking time or spending transport fare to visit the shop to go to shopping, shortening or reducing shopping time to do another important matter.

On conclusion, global many consumers began feel online shopping can bring more economic benefits on shortening shopping time, avoiding transport fare spending aspect. So, online shopping will be popular shopping behavior for future long time. It may encourage global many shoppers can make rapid shopping decision in short time in order to carry on any products buying transaction to global any one online shopper in short time easily in behavioral economic view. So, global many businessmen had begun to build themselves one attraction webstore in order to persuade different countries consumers to choose to click themselves webstores from internet channel to buy any kinds of products in short time easily.

So, internet technology had changed consumers traditional shopping behaviors to build positive online shopping emotion as well as raise online sellers‘ any products sale chance easily in behavioral economic view.

Why and how human behavior may influence the country's economic growth or recession?

When one country has many people choose to do the same matter for

one period, whether their behavior may influence the country's pvera; economic growth or recession . I shall attempt to indicate cases toexplain their relationship as below:
For flowing rubblish behavioral case example, do you feel that when the country has many people often flow rubblish on the streets, instead of their flowing rubblish behavior may bring streets dirty? But, their flowing rubblish behavior may explain that this country has people may have enough money to buy food to ear, or enough cloths to wear, enough bottles of water to drink, even they may have enough money to buy new television, radio, refrigeraters , washing machines, desktops or laptops electronic home products from old to new to use in order to satisfy their living needs. So, when they flow old electronic home products, their flowing old home electronic products behaviors may seem that they have enough money to buy other new home electronic products to replace old home electronic products to use at homes.
However, it seems thaat this country ought have many people have jobs to do. So, many of them, they can easy to make purchase decison to flow any old home electronic products and buy any new home electronic products to use . Because this country has many people have jobs to do. So, they can often not use old home electonic products to become rubblishs to flow on streets after they had bought any kinds of new home electronic homes.
In fact, it also implies that this country's economy grows rapidly. So, many businesses can glow up rapdly. When they expanded their businesses, they must need to increase employees number in order to let they help themselves to raise productivity or serve their clients absolutely. So, when the country has many businesses can grow up, it seems that its economy must be better or it is improved to compare past. Due to many different kinds of home electronic products had been often bought to use by this country people in this period. So, this country's any streets can be observed that expensive electronic home products were flowed on streets anywhere. then, this country will have many electronic home products sellers can sell their home electronic products very easily. When this country has many people can find any kinds of jobs to do easily. So, due to unemploymen rate had been decreasing.
In behavioral economic view, as this many electronic home products rubblish country case, we can observe this country may have many people have jobs to do. So, consumption number has been increased long time. So, cheap food, or expensive home electronic products may be rubblish on

any streets. This country's people , their flowing rubblish behaviors may be explained that many of people have enough jobs to do, so they have ability to buy any good taste food to eat or buy any kinds of expensive electronic home products to use. So, this country's economy may be improved for this long period. So, in behavioral economic view, when this country can have many electronic home products rubblishs are flowed on anywherer in streets frequently. It seems that this country will have many people have jobs to do, so it causes they often change old home electronic products or replaced them easily, when they have enough income to spend to buy any kinds of new home electronic products to use at homes easily. Moreover, their flowing old electronic home products behaviors also indicate that this country has many people their salaries may be increased in possible from their emplyers. When this country can have many different kinds of home electornic products are sold. It means that this country's electronic home products needs or demand had been increasing, due to many people have jobs to do and income increases to excite their living of needs also improve. Consequently, this country may seem have better economic improvement. We can observe from this country's electronic home products rubblish increasing income in theis period.

On conclusion, this country ought experience economic growth at this period. So, " flowing expensive electronic home rubblish increasing number " may seem that this country's economic growth is rapidly in this period, due to many people have jobs to do as well as salaries increase in this period.

Technology how impacts human behavior changing?

Technology how influences human behavior to bring changing? For example, online share purchase and sale transaction from smart phone brings share investor can do share buying or selling transation in any where and any time conveniently, non manual driving auto vehicle, bring car owner feels comfortable and spends free time to do other matter, e.g. reading, listening mucis in himself or herself car freely. electrical energy vehicle can help car owner to reduce air polluton and it can brings the drivers do not feel drive long time in any journeys in order to avoid air pollution for environmental protection responsible car drivers in our societies. Thus, they will drive long time in any journeys when they can drive electronic energy cars to replace oil energy cars.

However, online technology can also bring consumers can choose to stay at homes to buy any things from seller individual online webstore conveniently. Such as online technology can bring shoppers do not need to spend much time to visit shops to buy any things. They can choose any kinds of products from any online sellers individual online webstores conveniently at homes. Online technology excite busy consumers can make purchase decision easily as well as it can help online sellers sell any kinds of products from internet easily.

In behavioral economic view, technology can change human behavior to be improved, it can let human feels comfortable, more free time ro use, rapid making any decisions, such as apply smart phones to make share purchase or sale transaction decision, online shopping decision, even travelling any where decision in short time, when the traveller finds the most cheap hotel accommodation room price and air ticket price frm any travel agent online tourism webstore, then the potential travel customer can follow the online hotel accommodation price and air ticket price data to make decision when to buy the air ticket from the airline travel agent or make decision when to prebook which hotel accommodation room to go to the country to travel from online travel agent tourism webstores. So, technology can encourage global any country travelers to make anywhere to trvel rapidly. If the traveler can find the country's general hotel rooms and airline tickets prices had been decreasing more sightly. The traveler may make travel decision to choose the country to travel in short time, then he/she can prebook the country;s any hotel room and airline ticket to pay by visa fraom the country's any hotel and airline travel agent webstores., before one week, even one month or more easily. Hence, online technology can also encourage traveler individual frequent travel times to be increased, due to global travelers can find any hotel rooms and airline tickets prices from internet conveniently at homes. They do not need to spend time to visit any airline travel agent to enquire travel choice country's hotel rooms prices and airline ticket prices. They can compare global travel of countries choices ' all hotels rooms and airline agents air tickets prices to make prebook airline seat and hotel room decision before one week, one month even six months early.

On conclusion, online technology can encourage global travelers can make travelling any where and when traveling time desicions easily. It can excite tourism industry develops in long time. Also, such as electricity cars invention can encourage environment protection car owners do car purchase decision easily, because they can choose to drive electronic energy cars to replace oil energy cars in order to avoid air pollution occurs easily.

So, electronic cars can increase electronic car purchasrs number, due to many of environmental protection attitude of car owners can choose to drive electricity cars to bring air cleans, even non -manual driving cars can encourage lazy driving and free time driving car owners to choose to buy non-manual (artificial intelligent) cars to drive , because they can spend much free time to read, listen music or do any matters in themselves cars, they do not need to drive cars, robotic (AI) auto driving machine is such one non-manual driver to help them to drive themselves cars confidently. So, non-manual driving cars can attract lazy and enjoying free time driving car owners to choose to buy to replace traditional manual cars to drive easily. Moreover, online share transaction can help any share investors to make share buying and selling decision in short time easily. When they can apply smart phones technological tool to carry on share buying and selling activities easily. They can observe any share rising or falling price suitation from smart phones in any where any any time easily. So, smart phone technology can help global any shareholders to make share purchase and sale transaction easily. So, technology can encourage human makes decision in short time rapidly.

How and why employees behaviors may influence economy development?

In behavioral economy view,I believe the country's any organizational employees behavior may bring indirect relationship to influence the country's long term economic development. I shall indicate past manufacture industry social development period to explain their relationship. For many countries' past business activities had belonged to manufacturing industry, such as US, UK past before 1980 year, it focused on steel manufacturing and steel manufacturing related machine products. So, US, Uk developed countries manufacturing industries may be past main country's economic income sources. I assume US , UK past had one million number different kinds of industries. They ought had about seven houndred thousand number organizational businesses were belonged to manufactured industry. They may include:

Steel manufacturing and steel related machine manufacturing, e.g. vehicle manufacturing, home appliances, e.g. washing machine, television, radio, refrigerate cooler, heater, air condition etc. different kinds of different kinds of steel -related manufacturing machine, they were manufactured from US, UK steel machine manufacturers. So, US, Uk the other three hundred thousand number industry may be general service industry, e.g. hotel service, restaurent, cinema, public transport service, tourism lesiure , wine bar, supermarket etc. different kinds of non-manufacturing industries business organizations were operated in UK, US past before 1980 year.

So, in UK, US developed countries industry development history, they ought have high percentage of businesses belonged to steel related manufacturing machine and steel products. Also, in the past before 1980 year, US, Uk business employers , they employed many workers are manufacturing workers. They needed to spend long time to work in factories. They were skillful workers, and they are trained to manufacturing cars, washing machine, television, heater, etc. even steel itself different kinds of steel related products to prepare to deliver to their shops to sell to US, Uk local or overseas clients.

So, I believe that past UK, US ought employ many employees, they belonged to skillful manufacturing workers, manufacture increasing steel machine or steel related machine number of products rapidly daily. So, if UK, US had had many of these manufacturing factories owned high skillful workers, then their manufacturing steel-related machine or steel both kinds of products number must be influenced to raise rapidly. Consequently, their steel machine manufacturing products would been exported to overseas or would been sold to local both markets , they may be influenced to raise sale number. They (these manufacturing workers) needed to be trained to know how to manufactur these different kinds of machine products in the efficient teams and they ought to be trained to raise their efficiencies in order to shorten time to manufacturing many kinds of steel related manufacturing machine or steel itself products rapidly. So , if their efficiencies and manufacturing performance was improved, these US, UK any one manufacturing worker and their teams ought achieve raising productivities significantly.

Hence, when past UK, US manufacturing industry development period, if these two countries' any manufacturing factories could have many manufacturing workers could be trained to be skillful and proficient manufacturing workers. Then, in past every day to these factories workers, they ought help their steel or steel related manufacturing employers to raise any kinds of machine or steel products number in every team. So, when past in the manufacturing industry development, US, UK could have many factories' manufacturing workers themselves steel or steel related machine products manufacturing skill could be trained to to improve to any kinds of these machine or steel manufacuring products quality as well as

their products number could be influenced to raise by themselves skillful improvement significantly every day.
Then, what would be influenced to occur to past UK, US manufacturing industry period? In behavioral economic view, when these two manufacturing industry developed countries, such as UK, US , if they had many factories workers can be trained to improve their skill in order to achieve any kinds of steel or steel-related machine products quality could be improved as well as products manufacturing number could be also increased absolutely.
In consequence, past UK and US both countries ought increase themselves any kinds of steel and steel related machine products number to be supplied to themselves local shops to let local clients to choose any one kind of machine manufacturing products to buy easily as well as they could also export to supply overseas any countries to buy their different kinds of steel or steel related machine products to let overseas steel or steel related manufacturing machine product buyers, they can have many of these different kinds of these steel or steel-related different kinds of manufacturing machine from UK and UK these both countries easily to compare other countries.
On conclusion, I believe that past US, and UK macro manufacturing industry income GDP would increase significantly. So, they would have good economic growth performance because when many of these manufacturing workers themselves manufacturing effort could be improved. So, it explained when employees manufacturing abilities can influence economic growth indirectly.

Robots invention whether they can help organizations to raise efficiencies or inefficiencies?
In behavioral economic view, in any organizations, when the organization hopes its worker teams can raise efficiencies , the organization may choose to increase more workers number and/or it can provide training to improve these workets themselves skills in order to raise their efficiencies. For one warehouse example, when the warehouse increases many goods , they are needed to delivered these goods from the shelves to the delivering destination locations. If this warehouse supervisors feel these workers themselves goods delivery speeds are slow, which is possible due to this warehouse's workers number is not enough. So, this warehouse supervisor ought increase workers number in order to increase their goods delivery speed in order to deliver goods from the shelves to every indicated goods

delivery destination in order to let any one lorry driver can transport the right kinds of goods and ensure the accurate goods number to transport to any one client home rapidly.

However, if this warehouse supervisor planed to buy several warehouse goods delivery robots to assist these warehouse workers to find the right kinds of goods from shelves and then deliver to the right destination location in the warehouse. So, these warehouse orkers can concentrate on counting the accurate goods number and ensuring the right kinds of goods in order to prepare to let lorry drivers to transport these goods to these goods of buyers themselvers homes rapidly. Consequently, in the first step, robots can concentrate on finding th right goods from shelves and delivers them to the right goods transportation of location destination. Then, in the second step, these warehouse workers can concentrate on counting the accurate goods number and ensuring the right kinds of goods in order to prepare to put them to the lorry. Consequently, when warehouse robots and warehouse workers can cooperate to work together, the most important, robots, can deal on finding the right kinds of goods and deal on delivering the accurate number of goods of job duty as well as these warehouse workers can only concentrte on counting the right kinds of goods number in order to avoid it has none any mistake of wrong kinds of goods and inaccurate goods of delivery number to be transported to the lorry and to deliver to any one buyer's home.

So, it seems that warehouse robots ought help any one warehouse worker to raise himself efficiency and avoid goods delivery of mistake occurrence easily as well as their help to warehouse workers that can let any one goods buyer feels their goods can be delivered to their homes rapidly. Moreover, warehouse robots can also help these warehouse workers to raise efficiencies because warehouse robots can help them to shorten goods delivery time between any one shelf and any one goods delivery destination of location in the warehuse because robots may help them to find the right kinds of goods from the right shelf in the short time. So, any one worker does not need to spend long time to seek anywhere is the right shelf location for the kind of goods when the kind of goods are needed to deliver to the buyer's home from lorry. Warehouse robots can help them to do this aspect of " finding the goods from the right shelf in short time job duty". So, any one warehouse worker only needed tospend less time to do the counting of any right kind of goods number and ensuring the right kind of goods job duty. Consequently, this warehouse 's any one worker, his any one kind of goods delivery time may be reduced, because robots' assistance and they may have more confidence to avoid mistake to deliver the wrong number of goods and/or the wrong kind of goods to any one goods buyer's home.

On conclusion, it seems that warehouse robots ought may help any one warehouse worker to raise efficiency for any one team in the warehouse as well as the warehouse any one supervisor does not need to spend much time to observe any one worker individual performance for " goods delivery job duty aspect" because their goods delivery job duty that had been replaced to do by these several warehouse robots. Robots can achieve the more accurate of right kinds of goods and the right number of goods delviery job performance to compare any one of human warehouse worker themselves right kinds of goods of delivery and right number of goods of delivery job performance. So, when robots can participate to cooperate with this warehouse's any one worker to do their goods of delivery job duty in this warehouse every day. Then, robots can raies any one of supervisor individual confidence in order to let they do not need to spend time to observe any one of worker individual whose goods of delivery job performane. They can concentrate on supervising any one worker whose goods transport to lorry in the final step in order to avoid to deliver wrong goods number and / or wrong kind of goods to any one goods buyer's home every day. Consequently, this warehouse's overall teams of their delviery of goods performance many be improved by robotss' participatin to goods of delivery task as well as this warehouse's oveall teams themselves efficiencies may be influenced to raise by robots' goods of delivery task participation.

Why social behavior may influence organizational strategy needs to be changed ?

Why any organizations need to know whether nowadays social behaivor how has been changing in order to implement the kind of the most right strategy to achieve the profit aim pursue in possible. I shall indicate nowadays ecommerce or online, customer shopping behavior to explain above question concerns they ought have close relationship between social behavior and organizational strategic choice or organizational behavioral changing need.

On nowadays ecommerce business, or online shopping model, this kind of shopping model in global many young and old age consumers like to apply internet tool to choose any country sellers website stores in order to stay at home to buy any kinds of products from themselves webstores in global societies.

In fact, online shopping model had been popular for long time above to twenty years. Most of global sellers will make decision to design themselves webstores in order to attract global many online buyers to choose to buy their products from themselves webstores. So, it seems that social consumers purchase behaviors had been changed to online shopping from internet invention.

Hence, social consumers purchase behavioral changes may influence any organizations‘ strategies need to be changed from visiting shops purchase strategy model to online purchase strategy model, if the seller still concentrate on concentrate on considerate how to design itelf , but neglects to considerate how to design itself webstore, e.g. how to design attract product photos to put on itself webstore, how to arrange sale price information location to be putted on webstore and visa card payment location on itself webstore in order to let any one online buyer can feel very easier to buy itself any kinds of products from itself webstore. Then, its potential online buyers will be influenced to increase number when they can find this online seller itself any kinds of products photes and every kinds of product sale price information and visa card payment channel locations easily from itself webstore.

So, it implies that nowadays any one seller ought need to design one webstore to let any one online overseas and domestic consumers can have chance to click itself webstore to choose any one kind of product to buy conveniently when he/she does not hope to leave him/her home to go to shop, because nowadays social shopping behaviors had been influenced to change when internet invention, them it gives another online purchase method to replace visiting shops purchase method to global any one buyer in nowadays societies.

So, if nowadays any one seller still concentrate on how to design itself shop display in order to put any kinds of product on shelf in order to let any one visiting shop customer to find the kind of product to buy, but it neglects to change to choose to pursue another new technological shopping method, such as webstore purchase method in order to implement effective strategy to design the most right webstore as well as in order to attract global overseas and local consumers to find itself webstore easily from website and find its any one kind of product phots and sale price and visa card payment button in order to choose to buy itself any kinds of products in the short time. Consequently I believe that the seller will lose many customers from overseas and local when its other same or similar product sellers choose to design themselves webstores in order to let global any one product buyer can buy themselves any one kind of product when they can pay visa card to buy their products from them webstores conveniently when they stay at home habitly. Then, the seller will lose many global potential customers in long time.

On conclusion, in behavioral economic view, any consumer behavioral social changing, which will influence any in order to avoid customers number loses significantly . In future time, organizations need to make rapid decision in order to implement the most reasonable and the most useful strategy in order to avoid global potential customers number reduces or lose them in long time. So, social behavioral changing environment ought influence any global organizations need to decide how to change themselves strategies in order to avoid customers loses significantly in future time.

How and why human behavior may influence economic growth or recession?

May ourselves daily behaviors influence our global societial continue economic growth or recession? Do they have cause and effect close relationship between human behaviors and global economic growth or recession? I shall apply behavioral economic theory to analyze and explain whether ourselves daily behaviors and our global societial economic growth or recession which have close cause and effect relationship as below:

Every country itself economic development must depend on any business activities, otherwise, any kinds of business activities must need ourselves business activities or behaviors in order to achieve any business activities as well as achieve the country's overall economic development in macro view. However, any country's overall business activites or behaviors which must depend on any kinds of individual businessmen, themselves employees daily working behavior or activity or performance in order to help them to attract or increase many clients number to acieve " earning profit" aim. So, it seems that any individual business, itself overall every department individual working behavior is one main factor to influence the company's overall business performance.

For agricultural fruit and meat food farming industry example, such as New Zealand is a farming main target industry country. It had had many New Zealanders were daily themselves own farming businesses for many years. Their farming businesses include growing fruit, sheep, cow, pig pork, meat etc. food sale business. If the New Zealand farmer owned a large size farming land, then he will choose either growing fruit or feeding sheeps, pigs, cows to be meat to to transport to New Zealand supermarkets to help them to sell to their farmers meet to New Zealanders in order to earn profit. Thus, if the New Zealand farmer owned large size of farming lands, then he needs to employ many farming employees (farming workers) to help him to carry on farming business daily tasks, e.g. picking up friuts, feeding pigs, cows, sheeps to eat food daily. These daily farming jobs are very important to influence this New Zealand farmer's meats or fruits sale number whether they can be easy or diffcult to sell in New Zealand supermarkets , if these farming workers can own encough farming knowledge or skill to know how to pick up fruits method and make judgement to know whether it is right time to pick up the kind of fruits from the trees , as well as know how feed this pigs, sheeps, cows to eat food in order to let they are better health. Consequently, their farming behaviors which can let these animals can provide the best taste and enough meat from these animals to let New Zealander to buy to eat from New Zealand any one supermarket. Even these New Zealand farming workers can know whether the kinds of fruits, e.g. oranges, apples, gapes etc. fruits whether they ought be picked up from the trees at the right time. Consequently, they can make judgement to decide to pick up any kinds of the best taste fruits to let any one New Zealander to buy to eat from any one supermarket in New Zealand. Otherwise, if they do not make judegement to know whether the kind of fruit ought not be picked up because they still need longer time to continue grow up to increase fruit size and better taste from the trees in order to let any one fruit buyer can feel better taste when they eat this kind of fruit later. If they can buy this kind of fruit to eat later, then this New Zealand farmer's his fruit buyers can buy the best taste of this kind of fruit to eat from an yone supermarket in New Zealand. Consequently, many New Zealand supermarkets will choose to buy any kinds of fruits from this farmer fruit supplier when they feel this farmer's fruits can provide more better taste fruits to compare other farmers' fruits.

Thus, due to New Zealand is one farming main income source country. It's any kinds of fruits and meats need to be export to overseas to sell , instead of local sale. It's GDP percent is very high to whole country 's overall income source. So, any one New Zealand farmer individual and any one farming worker individual working behavior will influence its economy whether it is influenced to grow or recession possible. Moreover, it also seems that farming workers' farming knowledge and skill will influence themselves farming daily activities to achieve the aim of the number of increase or decrease to any kinds of fruits whether they are better taste or the number of increase of decrease to any kinds of meats whether they are better taste to supply to any one New Zealand fruit or meat buyers to eat from any one New Zealand supermarket. So, it implies that any one New Zealand farming worker individual farming behavior may influence any kinds of fruits or any kinds of meat taste because they are transported to any one supermarket to sell in New Zealand.

Consequently, if New Zealans had many farmers can teach god farming knowledge and skill to let their any one farming workers know how to decide judgement to decide when it is right time to pick up any kinds of fruits from trees , or how to grow them on soil in order to let they can grow rapidly. Then, many different kinds of fruits can be provided to let any one New Zealanders can eat the best taste of fruits when their fruits are supplied to any one New Zealand supermarkets. Even, if they knew how to feed foods to pigs, cows, sheeps to eat daily. Then they can be more health and they can provide the best taste of meats to let any one New Zealanders can buy their meats from any one New Zealand supermarkets. Moreover, their fruits and meats can be transported to overseas to let any one country fruits or meats buyers can choose any kinds of New Zealand meats and fruits to buy to eat from themselves countries supermarkets. Then, many overseas fruit and meat buyers will perfer to choose New Zealand any kinds of fruits or meats to buy to compare other countries fruits or meats to buy when they go to any one local supermarkets.

On conclusion, it seems that New Zealand farming workers themselves farming behavior may influence their farming employers any kinds of fruits or meats sale number and income because their farming task behaviors must influence whether their fruits or meats taste are the better taste or worse taste to compare their other local farmers (the farmer competitors) whose fruits or meats taste. If tthe farmer's any one farming worker can be trained to learn how to know to feed animals skill and when is the most right time to pick up any kinds of fruits from trees or how to grow them on the soil methods. Due to these farming worker individual farming behavior may influence his different finds of fruits and meats sale number to be increase or decrease, so these any one New Zealand farmer must need to depend on any one farming worker whose farming working methods, if their farming working behaviors can be the best to influence any kinds of fruits to grow rapid or any kinds of pigs, cows, sheeps animals grow up rapidly , then their sale number may be increase significantly and their taste can be improved to let any New Zealand or overseas meat or fruit buyer to buy to eat to feel from any one New Zealand or overseas supermarkets, then New Zealand's agriculture industry must be influenced to increase. In the world, any one fruit or meat buyer must choose to buy New Zealand's fruit and meat to eat in prefer to compare other countries' fruits and meats. So, New Zealand's GDP may be influenced to raise from any one New Zealand farming worker individual farming working behaviors. It seems that New Zealand farmer fruit and meat sale number is depended on their eatting consumers demand more than their meat and fruit supply because if these NZ farmers can apply high technology method to grow good taste fruit or feed good taste meat to let global eatting customers to feel, their demand will increase, then NZ farmers will need to increase good taste fruit and good taste meat supply number to satisfy global meat and fruit eatting customer taste need.

CHAPTER SIX

What factors influence oil price changes

How the price of oil changes influences global tourism industry growth orrecession?

In macro-economic view, sudden mid and long term oil price shock can influence global torusim industry growth or recession. For example, a oil price of US$180 per barrel was considered only a few years ago, now this has a realistic scenario to which all plaers in the T&T sector have to adapt. At such a high level, the price of oil will become even more critical to almost every part of the tourism value chain. Although, weak global demand, caused by global economic recesson, resulted in a steep oil price decline to US$45 per barrel by the fourth quarter of 2008 in the past low oil price occurrence history, this won't change the mid to long -term oil forecast.

In fact, the past oil price occurrence history of the dramatic structural had changed a high price imposed on airlines, travelers, and destination countries, all of which will have to navigate through times of shifting or even declining travel demand. I assume that a high oil price scenario is assumed in the long term in order to highlight the changes , such a senario would mean for consumer behavior and the competitiveness of several destinations.

Low oil price in the 1970 and early 1980 did not bring significant growth of international air travel, but its growth has been strongest between 1980 and 2004, a period with stable and relatively moderate oil prices. Also, the rapid development of the low-cost carrier business model in the 1990s further fueled air travel growth by capturing tourism leisure demand , such as weekend leisure travel to cities using mostly secondary airports in any big area countries, such as UK, US . However, the tourism growth is whole influenced by high oil prices, due to oil price had been continue rising in possible.

Basis of oil is shortage supply product, oil is assumed to be the main energy source for the aviation sector for the nest 30 years. Although, second-generation biofuels seem to be on the horizon, the economics as well as the production scalability and aviation biofuel shortage will be a main challenge to airline industry. So, I assume that oil price will continue rise up, if there have none any aviation biofuel can be reflected to oil to use for air plane energy.

Until 2004, the only factors to have affected air travel growth, negatively were in external shocks , such as 9/11, causes catching air plane crisis or US regional geopolitical conflicts. It brings some travelers feel fear to go to US travel, as well as until recently 2019, human mouth disease can influence air to have disease to anyone from mouth. So, global travelers number had been continue decreasing, because they are fear to get disease by air when many themselves every stranger travelers are sitting on the without windows air planes. Although, mouth human and air disease and US 9/11 air attack both matters may influence oil price falls effect, because air planes flying times will reduce. They won't need frequent to fly, to cause aviation oil energy need reduce. Consequently, oil price will decrease, due to travelers number reduces and air planes flying times are also influenced to reduce. (oil demand decreases cause oil price decrease). Although, air lines ' cost will also be influenced reduce, but oil price decrease can not bring travelers number increase , when air ticket price reduce because global many leisure and business trip travelers feel fear to catch air planes frequently when human mouth air disease occured in 2019. So, oil price decreases can not grow up tourism industry growth or rise tourism income.

However, the obvious impact of a high oil price is an increase in the operating costs of airline. Moreover, fuel cost as a percentage of airline operating costs vary significantly based on the length of the flight. The longer the flight, the higher the fuel costs as a percentage of the airline operating cost. So, from an online's perspective, long -hauel flights represent the most criticial challenge to profitable operation because the share of fuel on these flights, compared with other cost items, is largest, because of the unfacorable fuel economics, due to fuel costs even at high-load factors. For example, Thai airways dropped its non-stop Bongkok to US flights in the summer of 2008 for commercial reasons, because fuel reached operating cost levels of 55 percent on this route, a cost burden that could not be passed on to their customers. So, the estimated price elacticity of passengers demand at this Bongkok to US flights route is high, if Thai Airways rises less air ticket price, it will influence many travelers to choose other airlines to catch air plan to fly. Hence, due to Thai Airways can not make decision to rise air ticket price, because it believes that it will lose many travelers, so it only chooses to drop this non-stop Bongkok to US flights to avoid fuel cost rising economic loss.

However, although micro and macro economic theories may also that oil price variable or change, it may influence global tourism income. But, recently, on 2019, human mouth and air diseases, it can influence global individual leisure and business trip travelers feel fear to catch air plans to avoid their bodies get this kind of death sickness when they sit in the no fresh air supplying air planes. They feel that they reduce leisure travelling flying times or business trip flying times with strange travelers to sit in crowd air planes together. Then, they must many avoid human moth and air disease to avoid death crisis. Hence, in this global human mouth and air diseases threat environment occurrence, even oil price sudden reduces to low price, it brings airline's cost reduces and air ticke price reduces. However, when air ticket price reduce to be very cheaper, it can not still attract global many leisure or business trip travelers to buy air tickets to fly frequently. Why does air ticket reduction, it can not attract many leisure or businee trip travelers to buy air ticket to fly ? The main reason is because human mouth and air disease influences global many travelers feel fear to catch air planes frequently. In psychological view, this kind of human mouth and air sickness will bring long time negative influence to global traveles do not want to catch air planes for business trips or travelling leisure frequently. So, it implies that oil price changing to influence air ticket price reduction factor ought not main factor to influence tourism income. It may include traveler individual negative emotion psychological factor, such as human mouth and air disease or 2019 9/11 attack both cases, they can influence global travelers feel fear to catch air planes to fly to avoid death threat. So, oil changing price ought not be only one absolute main factor to influence global tourism income significantly.

On conclusion, in economic view, it seems that oil chang price may have indirect or direct relationship to influence tourism income, instead of some unpredicted external environment factors influence, such as US 9/11 attack crisis and human mouth and air disease factors, they may be main factors to influence travellers number to reduce in non-economic external unpredicted environment view.

How did First World War influence Europe economy and tourism industry declines ?

Can wars bring either advantages or disadvantages or both to impact our economy growth ?In history, I feel that international war can influence any country's economy development has either positive or negative impact in possible.

On the inflationary hand, for the First World War economy growth influence example, in the First World War and since most notably the German hyperinflation of the 1920 year, this type of monetary regime shows a far smaller tendency towards inflation. In the First World War period, volatility of inflation and output were higher in the short run. So, First World War had little negative impact to influence world inflation in the war period. However, in the First World War period, the supply of money was determined not by the rates of economic growth only, but by the amount of available gold and could not be adjusted in response to economic needs. So, new sources of gold would increase money supply and inflation and decrease interest rates , the opposite of what modern central banks would do to provide stable economic growth in First World War. So, it explained that the First World War occurrence caused the change from non-inflationary to inflationary long term development. Thus, it seems First World War brings more money supply and gold supply to stable economic growth in the future long term period.

On the labor productivity influence hand, leaving monetary issues aside, the First World War created the working time intellectual mood to change labor productivity, it would be a 15-18 hours working week for more enlightened leisure to Europe labors. Some prominent modern economists on the accuracy of the predictions on GDP growth per capital was remarkably accurate given to be fallen down that it was made at the time when economy growth theory did not even exist in the First World War period. Thus, it seems First World War also causes working time to be raised to the developing countries during the industrialization period. Then, the long time working time brought to the developing countries' workers to it is poor for labor health. Hence, although employers can raise productivity, but they need many workers to work long time to cause unhealthy. The majority found that the prediction on leisure is of the variations between world regions , due to income level exist, making European variety of capitalism. So, the First World War caused income inequality within countries and between nation states, trends in working hours , world poverty and ever growing needs (consumerism) and the like. Thus, the developed western countries' workers can work lesser time to compare to the developing Asia countries' workers. Consequently, First World War brought negative impact to influence the developing Asia countries' worker unhealthy and physical and mental illnesses number had been increasing as well as it brought positive impact to influence the labor productivity had been increasing to the Asia countries' employers, due to their workers need to work long time every day.

It seems on the positive impact hand, that the First World War caused the inflation occurrence to bring more money supply and gold supply to be raised to influence global economic growth. But, on the negative impact hand, it also brought low working hours in European developed countries and high working hours to the Asia developing countries which are needed to do different occupations in developing countries as well as the income inequality caused unfair social challenge had also occurred in developed countries, such as Europe, UK, US etc. and developing countries, such as China, Japan, Korea etc . Thus, First World War had brought developed countries better economy development and better salary and less working hours to labors because Europe had reached the mature stage of industrialization to avoid labors who needed to work overtime. Otherwise, it had brought developing countries poor economy development and poor salary and labors need work long time to raise productivities.

In conclusion, it implied that the First World War had bought some bad influences to developing countries' economic system, e.g. social income inequality, working hours inequality, inflation and GDP per capita going down in the past Europe economic history development, but it also bought welfares to developed countries' European labor working time intellectual mood to change labor productivity, it would be a 15-18 hours working week for more enlightened leisure to Europe labors. So, it seemed to cause negative economic influence to developing countries, but it cause positive economic influence to developed counties during the First World War time.

CHAPTER SEVEN

MTR catching time reducing ticket price raising strategy

How underground train MTR can let passengers to feel catching time reducing to raise fare competitive effort?

It has close relationship between globalization and global tranport development. How globalisation impacts on the environment via changes taking place in the transport sectors. In fact, it is not clear how the relative price changes that result from openness will affect the environental composition of economic activity. For example, some countries will produce more environmentally intensive goods, others will produce fewer. On the other hand, liberalisation will raise incomes, perhaps increasing the willingness to pay for environmental improvement. These potential income effects increased outweigh the negative scale effects with increased economic activities. When combined with the positive effects with technology transfer, the net effect on local pollutants could be positive . Hence, we need to find methods to solve the problem of raising transport economic activities and serious environmental pollution creating as the same time occurrence.

Globalisation helps to facilitate greater division of labor, and to exploit its comparative advantage more completely. In longer term, globalization also stimilates technology an dlabour transfers, and allows the dynamism that accompanies economic activities to stimulate the development of new transport technologies and short time transport processes that lead to global welfare improvement.

On shipping transport industry aspect, shipping will increase ocean pollution, when international shipping activities are increasing. Trade and shipping encourages energy use in shipping is coupled with the movement of waterborne commerce. The estimates depending on the transport goods number of at-sea or in port days much increase globally every day. The energy demand of international shipping fuel sale number and domestically assigned fuel sales number also increases for global fuel usage. Estimates of ocean going ships now consume about 2% to 3% and perhaps even as much as 4% of world fossil fuels.Hence, when global shipping energy fuel usage number increases, because global shipping trading activities number increases. It will bring the environmental pollution to ocean level increases. On air transport industry aspect, their travellers' catching air plans travelling needs and businesses' goods transport air delivery service needs are increasing from the requirements for high quality , fast and reliable international transport. Moreover, the networks that airline companies operate have changed often to hub-and spoke networks, many new often low -cost companies have entered the air freight market, any long time air journey is needed, e.g. Australia airline expands its one new air journey flies to UK, it needs two days flying time. It means that every flight to UK from Australia , it needs to use more fuel to fly. Then , air pollution will increase also.

On road transport industry aspect, global road transport cost and transit times, traffic jam occurrence chances also increase because when the road building number is increasing globally. So, it will cause traffic jam and long journey time spending , even fuel usage spending number is also increased. Then, accident occurrence chance is raised. Hence, global business or entertainment transport activities number increasing , it will bring much negative impact on environmental pollution, traffic jams number increases, long journey spending time increases, fuel usage number increases. Although , frequent transport activities may bring GDP income.

On transport service industy aspect, but is also brings negative influence to standard of living. It means that when transport fuel demand increases, transport activities number increases, GDP income on relative any transport activities needs industy , e.g. logistic demand needs, when lorry drivers need to drive lorries to deliver goods from one warehouse to another warehouse or supermarket or office etc. different business places on the road driving activities increase. But, it also bring air pollution , traffic noise and traffic jam etc. transport problems to road and natural environment and raises worse standard of living , bad emotion to working people or learning emotion to students , due to frequent traffic jam causes , low efficiency and productivity to workers, even student individual learning time can be reduced if they need to spend long time to wait bus, ferry, rail, underground train to go to schools , due to frequent long time traffic jam occurs on the roads to influence they can not go to schools on time often when they are catching buses to go to schools absolutely in busy transport time.

Thus, although any countries need to consider how to design their transport system, e.g. how to e.g. how to choose the right locations to build roads to let many cars can be driven available easily when the morning and evening (office and school transport busy time, e.g. 6:00 to 9:00 AM morning, 6:00 to 9:00 PM in the evening transport time usually because these two transport periods are usually , there are many students and working people need to catch any public transportation or drive cars tools to go back homes. So, enough roads number and long and not narrow road area must be needed to design in order to let enough cars be driven on the roads in the transport busy times to the countries have many big cities or have high population , such as UK, US, China, India, Hong Kong. They have many people , but drivers and cars numbers both are increasing. So, efficient road design and road number are also needed to increase in order to let drivers can transport goods to deliver, students and working people can catch any public transport tools to arrive any destinations on reads in the short time rapidly in order to avoid to spend long time transportation time and late to arrive any destinations in possible occurrence. So, any sudden traffic jam is not hoped to be caused by easy traffic accidents occurrence any time.

Hence, global efficient road transport system is needed, when global transport activities are increased, because any road logistic transport activities are increasing, they will also influence the students and working people when they also need to catch any public transport tools or drive themselves cars to go to working places or schools on the roads at the same busy transport time between 6:00 to 9:00 AM morning busy transport time and between 6:00 to 9:00 PM evening busy transport time. Because these both times will be have many students, working people , they need either go to offices or schools or go to homes. Hence, if the country had many lorry drivers need to drive their lorries to deliver goods on the roads in the transport busy morning or evening time in the same driving time on the roads. It will increase the risk to cause frequent traffic jam or traffic accident occurrence easily in possible in the country. So, any countries' governments can not neglect how to design roads and choose anywhere are the roads suitable locations to be built as well as anywhere land useful number to build road location choices in order to solve geographical traffic jams occurrence chance.

Hence, globalization of transport activities may bring geographical GDP growth, but it also bring traffic jams and traffic accidents occurrences, hearing impairment due to traffic noise, air pollution, traffic crashed, bad working emotions to workers and bad learning emotions to students, due to spending long transport time when traffic jam or traffic accidence occurs more easily.

However, transportation is an important tool if a country's progress. Rapid economic growth and increasing level of urbanization enhances a person's living standard have, it leads to a greater travel demands. Hence, governments ought not neglect have to design its roads , measure every road's length or width whether it has how many cars need to drive in morning or evening transport busy time for students, working people and delivery goods drivers of public transportation tools or private transportation tools easy driving needs in order to avoid frequent traffic jams or traffic accidents occurrences in possible.

Moreover, any governments also need to solve these issues, if they hope to develop their transport system successfully. These issues include : What mode of transportation to cost-effective in meeting a region's transportation needs to the country? How should a state department of transportation prioritize its highway delivers to maximize economic growth? What is the trade-off between additional growth in urban area and the cost of expanding transportation systems to accommodate greater growth? What effect does the expansion of transportation systems have on the need to invest in other types of transport modes? For example , the transport expansion may include the construction of additional highway segments, rail lines, runways, or additional sea, air, rail or bus terminal capacity using traditional technology; highway may include the additional of lanes to an interstate highway system; the conversion of an existing two-lane road to a four lane limited access highway, replacement or widening of bridges, and the extension of an existing road. Airport examples, include runway lengthening, apron expansion, and additional terminal gates.

On the other hand, enhancement to new transport technologies may bring efficiency of the existing highway system, examples may include intelligent highway systems, congestion pricing, intermodal freight facilities, geographic positioning systems, and instrument landing systems to mention of a few major transport innovations. So, transport policy makers need to understand the effects of these new transport mode innovations on economic development or GDP growth on transport activities growth transportation services and a more efficient use of limited land supplying scarce resources , air quality ,and noise pollution, traffic jams, long spending transport time to students, working people, entertaining people, even deliver goods lorry drivers their every day essential driving activities or catching public transportation tools needs problems. For example, the concept of intelligent highway systems needs increase trend. In simply , vehicles are being linked to each other and to traffic control devices to improve the efficiency of the total highway system. Similar types of innovations in intelligent traffic management are increasing needs for air, sea, and rail systems. The question is that whether intelligent highway systems can attribute of highways on economic development, raising on productivity of reducing highway congestion or improving pavement condition.

In fact, many developed countries' transportation system is mature. The nation has gone beyond the frontier of building, the interstate highway system and connecting most cities (markets). Tweaking the system with additional lanes and the new intelligent highway systems are useful in China, US, UK, because they have many cities. SO, road efficient traffic congestion control is needed when many students, working people, delivery goods transport people need to drive cars or catch cars on every city's roads in the transport busy time between 6:00 to 9:00 AM morning transport busy time as well as between 6:00 to 9:00 PM evening transport busy time.

However, transportation investment must be needed, if the country hoped to have good economic productivity, efficient transport service can bring good effects on the flows goods and people on roads every day when they use the country's transport system. So, any countries need to collect data, they can not be lack of enough transport information in any time that links anywhere locations of any drivers to the locations of the transport system that provide them with services in any time, e.g. every day morning and evening transport busy time, radio can report the real transport time of any roads traffic jam or traffic accident message to let drivers to listen to know whether anywhere roads are occurring traffic accidents or traffic jams or when the road traffic accident or traffic jam is solved to let the drivers can know whether when the roads can be opened to drive again. So, real time road transport message information is needed to report by radio, in order to let any drivers to know whether they ought choose to drive themselves cars on the road when they need to choose anywhere road to drive to the destination if they can know when the road has traffic accident or traffic jam occurs. They won't drive their cars on the road in the moment immediately.

On conclusion, globalization can being frequent transport economic activities. So, road , air, sea, transport service users' transport service needs are also increased. Every country ought not neglect how to innovate their transport service in order to satisfy their transport needs to achieve economic growth, efficient and short transport time spending, productivities increase, reducing air pollution, traffic noise , raisins standard of living on transport influence aspect to satisfy working people, students, entertaining people, delivery goods transport users' efficient road transport time behavioral spending aspect.

On conclusion, when one country's electric public transport tool service increases, it may cause gas need decreases and gas business will experience decline stage cycle stage rapidly.

CHAPTER EIGHT

How immigration and climate change influences general social sale increases

How immigration influences the country demand increases and general social sale price increases when the country's people number is increasing?

What are immigration impacts to social econoomy? Immigration how influences into a region impacts house prices in three ways. For a fixed level of local population, housing demand rises due to the increase in foreign-born population. In addition, immigrants can influence native location decisions and induce additional shifts in house demand.

Does immigration cause housing prices to be higher ? In applied economic view, economists determined that illigration contributed to no more than 0.1% to 0.12% increase in housing prices. Furthermore, an increase in new housing construction in response to higher demand also moderated the effect of immigration.

What impact did immigration have on society? The available evidence suggests that immigration leads to more innovation, in better educated workforce, greater occupational specialization, better working of skills with jobs, and higher overall economic productivity. Immigration also has a not positive effect on combined local budgets.

How does overpopulation affect housing by increasing immigrant number? Population change leads to a changing demand for housing population growth, and particularly the growth in the number of housing population growth, and particularly the growth in the number of households leads to a growth in hosing demand. Population decline might in the long term, leads to a decrease in housing demand.

However, immigration also brings good aspect to economy, instead of netagive aspect. The available evidence suggests that immigration leads to more innovation, a better educated workforce, greater occupational specialization, better matching of skills with jobs, and higher overall economic productivity. Immigration boosts the well-being of the society. If the growth rate of per-capita income increases thanks to immigrants, the standard of living of the general population can rise. For canada exampls, immigration can bring positive impact to Canada's economy. The 2026 census found that immigrants had median earnings of $29,770 compared to $36,300 for native born Canadians. Recent immigrants are far more likely than native born canadians to initially have low incomes, with income and employment rates increasing towards the national average with more than spent in canada.

What are the positive or negative impact to immigration? The channels have both positive and negative static and dynamic effects. One netagive static effect of immigration is that migration directly reduces the available supply of labour, particularly skilled labour, but these are positive static effects , such as through return migration and remittances.

The positive impacts of migration may include the opportunity to get a better job, improved quality of life, safety from conflict. The opportunity of a better education. The negative impacts of migration may include: Poverty makes them unable to live a normal and healthy life. Children growing up in pvoerty have no access to proper nutrition, education or health. Migration increased the slum areas in cities which increase many problems, such as unhygienic conditions, crime, pollution etc.

How does migration affect the economy in global? The available evidence suggests that immigration leads to more innovation, a better educated workforce, greater occupational specialization, better matching of skills with jobs, and higher overall economic productivity. Moreover, immigration also have has a not positive effect on improving productivity to the country's manufacturers aspect, for example, labour migrants have the most positive impacts on either positive or negative terms. The impact is negative, it brings small impact of the human capital brought by migrants on skillful manufacturing jobs aspect. As the same time, emigration can have a positive impact on development. Positive impacts on host countries, reducing job vacancies number and improving skills by overseas skillful immigrants. Also, returning migrants can bring savings, skills and international contacts.

Hence, the economic effects of migration, it indicates that high skilled migrants bring diverse talent and expertise, when foolish or poor skillful workers are improved or upgrade high skill and has no negative efffects on public fiances as immigration is found to have an overall positive impact on economic growth in long term. Moreover, the positive impact not just on population growth. Many migrants bring higher education and skill. The expanded attributed allow the modeling to better capture both the positive and negative impacts.

On conclusion, migrants have positive impact on developing countries called " how immigrants contribute to developing countries economies, e.g. leading a greater cultural diversity, social benefits, raising economic costs to manufacturers, e.g. reducing manufacturing cost, assisting refugees , e.g. households wealth, increasing due to they can find jobs to do easily when they emmigrate to the another country, such as migrant workers are an aset to the country where they bring their knowledge and skill to attribute to the new country's society. Hence, I think that immigration can bring many advantages to a country both for the economy and society as a whole.

Does health reason influence developing countries people to choose migration by climate change impact?

Climate change is caused substantial increases in population movement. It has considered the likely causal influences much movement and the risks to national and international security. But, there has been little research on the consequences of climate-related migration and the health of people who move. May health impacts of climate change play important role in population movement?

However, climate change-related migration is likely to result in adverse health outcomes, particularly in situations of forced migration. In fact, climate change is widely projected to cause substantial increases in the scale of human population movement. Forecasts of the number of people who will move by around midcentury in response to the effects of climate change vary from tens of millions to 250 million people (United Nations High Commissions For Refugees (UNHCR, 2009).

Many scientists believe migration reason is common that the countries' people are fear of diseases and climate change environmental disasters to be caused in their countries, especially developing countries by climate change negative influences. Specially, populations in low-income countries whose health is most at risk from climate changes and where. There are often high pre-existing levels of health problems are used to coping with adverse health outcomes without causing to migration. So, it is likely that population movement that is driven substantially by health risks will occur only where those risks are sufficiently serious and widespread. For example, Africa the country's climate change will bring the risk of infectious disease (e.g. cholera , measles, malaria, meningitis) to Africa. In fact, Africa has adequate health care systems, low immunization coverage, lack of clean water and poor sanitation (Zarocostas, 2011).

Thus, it seems that climate change will bring health rick challenge to the country to influence people to choose to migrate other countries. Although, the range and extent of health risks with future climate related population movements can't be clearly forever, but the evidence of health outcomes of movement of people indicates that health risks will predominate over health benefits. This often is an issue of considerable geopolitical, ethical and economic importance. Consequently, it has close cause and effect relationship between climate change and health risk to cause people to choose migration.

Impact of population growth and population ethics on climate change mitigation

Future population growth migration number is uncertain, due to climate change factor influence. Higher mitigation growth entails more emissions and means either more people will choose to mitigate other better climate countries to live or the better climate countries will have more people to immigrate to live, due to any sudden climate change environment related impacts.

However, some climate scientists feel how future population is related importantly determines mitigation decisions. They indicated that some bad climate countries' people make any mitigation decision choice, it responds to the fact that a larger population means climate change hurts more people. For example, in 2025 year assuming United Nations has high rather than low population scenario entails an increase in the social cost of carbon dioxide (SCC) of 85% under total utilitarianism (TU), vs 5% under average utilitarianism (AU). The difference is the (SCC) between the two population scenarios under (TU) is comparable to commonly debated decisions regarding time discounting. Additionally, they estimate the avoided mitigation costs implied by reductions in population growth, finding that large neat term savings US $6billions amount annually occur under (TU).

Hence, it seems that climate changing is one important factor to bring any bad climate change countries which need to pay large disaster expenditure to recover their economy after any sudden serious climate change impacts.

How climate change impacts on food price rises ?

In fact, climate change will increase global temperature change rainfall patterns and will result in more frequent and severe floods and drought. Depending on future emission of greenhouse gases, global temperatures are likely to rise between 2 degree and 4 degree within the next century. The main impacts of climate change will however not be felt through higher temperatures, but through a change in the hydrological cycle. Rainfall is likely to increase around the poles and the tropics when in the sub-tropics average precipitation is likely to decrease. Not only the average annual or seasonal rainfall will change, there also be an increase in the number of extreme events resulting in most frequent and severe floods and droughts.

How does climate change influence to development countries? Climate change will influence any development countries on these several aspects. They include as below:

On trade influence hand, reducing emission levels from the developing world is extremely important. If current developments are continuing, for example, emissions from China and India both countries will save be much higher than the total emission form all Europe countries. Currently, the Europe is stimulating mitigation and transfer of clean technologies through the clean development mechanism (CDM). Although, it is still unclear what the mitigation potential of the (CDM) is, especially in India the investment is (CDM) projects is significant. However, the Europe should take a much wider approach. In developing countries a lot can be done in terms of increasing energy efficiency, land use change and agriculture. It is also important that developing countries are stimulated to choose a sustainable, low emission developed pathway. Choices for more sustainable, low emission technologies should be made early in the process. It seems that climate changing will encourage many countries will choose to do more environment protection related trading, e.g. researching how to invent environment protection new products to reduce our earth pollution between European and any developing countries, such as China and India etc.

On focus mitigation efforts in least developed countries on land use change, agriculture development aspect, in the least developed countries mitigation efforts should not focus on the energy or transport sector, but on agriculture and forestry. Agriculture is responsible for a relatively large percentage of the emissions in many developing countries, e.g. Africa, China, Malaysia, Hong Kong, Japan etc. In this sector there are many win options both reducing poverty and reducing greenhouse gas emissions. For example, improved water and nutrient management can sharply increase production efficiency and reduces at least the amount of emission per kg food produced. Agro-forestry reduces greenhouse gas emission through increased carbon storage and reduces poverty through diversifying the incomes of local communities.

However, in most developing countries, the main limitation in coping with the impacts of climate change is a lack of capacity. Besides a lack of capacity, in many developing countries, there is also a significant lack of data and knowledge on climate change impacts. Developing countries should be stimulated to improve data gathering and make existing data more easily available.However, no migration effort will stop the need for adaptation. Especially, the least developed countries, who have contributed little to the problem will suffer the most.

On business strategies for climate change aspect, nowadays, the valuation for clean-technology companies, have increased considerable and the corporate carbon footprint has become an important topic to be discussed how to solve among senior managers? How can firms profit from what they do to address climate change? Thus, a low-carbon economy is already especially in energy, transport and heavy industry.

If current climate science holds true and there is considerable uncertainty in the estimates, global greenhouse gas emissions should ideally decrease from today's levels by 90 percent as of 2050 year in order to certain global warming below two degrees centigrade. Hence, it seems global warmth challenge brings further any new energy potential development businesses. Due to environment scientists encourage us to be realized the necessary increase in carbon productivity and new low-carbon technologies that are necessary dramatically reduces energy consumption and direct greenhouse gas emissions will have to be developed and then implemented widely to avoid future serious global environment warmth caused climate changes and pollution challenges occurrence.

What are the cause and effect economy relationship between climate change and environment migration to influence food sale price changes?

The choice of migration reasons can include that seeking better job chance, better job environment, better salary, better standard of life, better education, less crimes, feeling more safety etc. different psychological reasons. However, whether climate changing will be one factor to cause migration. This is one psychological life adaption issue. Some people may accept to adapt to live worse life when their countries are encountering any natural environment or economic negative or climate negative change or social negative impact suddenly. Otherwise, some people may not accept to adapt to live worse life when they countries are encountering any worse influences suddenly, such as sudden worse climate change. Thus, to research that whether it has relationship to influence migration choice between climate change and migration. We need to know whether what the general acceptable level to adapt climate change to human is.

It means that if the climate change has exceeded the countries' general people's acceptable level to adapt to live in their countries. Then, it is possible that it will cause many people do not feel more adaptive to live in their countries forever, due to serious sudden climate change disaster occurrence.

What is the general acceptable level to live to their countries to adaptive climate change? However, before they choose to migrate, they will mind these questions usually. How can they migrate? Once they leave, who will guard their land? How will they support their family in the city?

Environment problems are both sudden and gradual have always causal different formed of displacement around the world, but recent studied have emphasized that more people are likely to migrate in the future, owing to climate change (Stern, N. 2007).

In fact, climate change will bring serious challenge to any countries, such as natural resources shortage, lacking more productive livelihoods supply. Then, it views this question: If migration have no adaptive potential, then what can be done (or is being done) to facilitate communities to migrate? Analyzing

who migrants, how, why and where they go can provide useful insights for development planners aiming to support poor families. It seems that every family member's adaptive to live factor will influence the whole family who decides to choose to migrate or stay in their country when climate change disaster sudden occurs.

However, environmental migration is typically internal and short term, the potential for conflict is that unstable urban and rural demographics are related to higher risks of civil war and low level conflicts to environment migration during periods of environmental stress are common. Also, I believe that the impact of climate change can be divided into two distinct drivers of migration:

Climate processes driver , such as sea-level rise, shortage of agricultural land, desertification and growing water scarcity and climate events , such as flooding, storms. But, non-climate drivers, such as government policy, population growth and community level resilience to natural disaster are also important. All contribute to the degree of people's adaptive level.

The climate change problem is one of time (the speed of change) and scale (the number of people it will affect). Although, temporary migration is as an adaptive response to climate stress is already apparent in many areas. But the ability to migrate is a function of mobility and resources (both financial and social). IN other words, the people most to climate change are not necessary the one's most likely to migrate among of different migration factors.

In fact, predicting future flows of climate migrants is complex. Professor Myers' estimate of 200 million climate migrants by 2050 year has become the accepted figure-cities in respected publications from the IPCC to the Stern Review on the economics of climate change (Stern, N., Ed. 2006).Hence, it seems that there will have many different factors to cause climate migrant number rising in the future.

Consequently, migration and resettlement may be the most threatening short-term effects of climate change on human settlements. People may decide to migrate in any of the following cases. They includes: loss of housing (because of river, or sea flooding or mudslides), loss of living resources (like water, energy and food supply or employment affected by climate changes); loss of social and cultural resources (loss of cultural properties, neighborhood or community networks).

The three main climate change impacts to influence people to live may include that sea level rise: rising average sea level, sale water intrusion in aquifers, water availability (increase/decrease), extreme weather event: drought, heat waves, violent storms, floods. Thus, if any one of these environment change factors impacts to influence general people's life adaptive level to live anywhere in their any geographic location of their countries. Then, it is possible to influence them to choose to be environmental migrants. It means persons or group of persons who, for compelling reasons of sudden or progressive changes in the environment that adversely affect their lives or living conditions are obliged to leave their habitual homes, or choose to do so, either temporarily or permanently and who move either within their country or abroad. Thus, climate change can let them to feel that it is one unsafe natural disaster and it only brings negative effect to them when they still choose to live in their home town. It refers to situations where people are displaced across boarders in the context of sudden or slow onset disasters or in the context of the adverse effects of climate change.

In forces to non-forces mobility psychological view point, environmental refugee will have these three stages to decide migration: First stage is , refugee –like situation stage, it is very low level control over the whole process , vulnerability. Second stage is, environmentally driven displacement stage, it is compelled, but voluntary, more control over timing and direction and less vulnerability than refugees, but less control and more vulnerability than migrants. Final stage is migrant like situations stage, it is greater control over the process and less vulnerability , even if people are moving in response to deteriorating conditions (Hugo, G. 1996).

Consequently, climate change will be one main important factor to cause any country people who choose to do environmental migrants decision to compare other factors. IT seems, that climate change factor and environment migrant which have close relationship to cause any country people who choose to migrate more than social , economy , less crime, education, cultural , job change, standard of life etc. different external non-natural environment factors.

Climate change how influences global energy need ?

We are facing global warmth and natural resource and energy shortage challenges. Due to our Earth have limited natural resource numbers to supply to us to manufacture energy, but global population has been increasing every year. Thus, it is possible that we have energy shortage crisis. Also, manufactures are spending too much energy to waste to manufacture any products, the energy will cause air or water pollution in manufacturing process or drivers are driving their vehicles to pollute air on the roads. Then it will cause global warmth crisis. How we can avoid these both crises to occur. I shall give some recommendation as below:

Primary energy exploration method

● Greenhouse primary gas energy

Have you ever seen a greenhouse? A greenhouse can trap heat in the sunlight and keeps the air inside the greenhouse warm enough for plants to grow. The glass roof and walls of a greenhouse let in sunlight but prevent heat from escape, this makes the greenhouse warm inside. Similarly, some gases in the Earth's atmosphere can trap heat from the sun and keep the Earth warm. This is called the greenhouse effect. The gases energy that can trap heat from the sun are called greenhouse gases. It is future one kind of potential primary energy to reduce environmental pollution new energy products for human consuming.

● Underwater primary water energy

The world's underwater meeting took place around a table about five meters underwater. Many scientists believe that due to melting of ice caused by global warming, the sea level will rise by as much as 1 m by the end of this century. If the level of the sea rises in the future, most regions of the country will be underwater.

What impact of global warming is mentioned by underground water?

Can human apply underwater water technology to explore natural underground water energy to avoid global warming threat?

Why do we need to Safety in using fuel and handle gas leaks? Why do we feel town gas smell? How is electricity located at electric station far away from town area? How to solve problems caused by the use of fossil fuels? How to reduce the use of fossil fuels?

To solve the problems, the best way is to reduce our used of fossil fuel. This helps prevent fossil fuels form being used up too quickly. Also, it helps us to reduce environmental problems because fewer pollutants are given out when less fossil fuels are used. Can human help to reduce the use of fossil fuels? Fossil fuels are mainly in power station. Although we use some fossil fuels for our gas cooker and car, it won't make much difference if I use less.

Fossil fuel is not used renew primary energy. Most of energy we use come from fossil fuels, for example, the electricity we use is generated in power stations by burning fossil fuels. The buses we ride use diesel oil. Therefore, we can help reduce the use of fossil fuels by saving energy in our daily lives.

The actions that we can take such as: setting the air-conditioner to a higher temperature, walking instead of using lift, taking a short shower instead of a bath. This reduces the use of the hot water and thus the energy needed to heat the water. Thus, many people can help a lot to reduce our use of fossil fuels to avoid fossil fuel shortage risk occurrence.

For Hong Kong people energy consumption case, how much energy is used when a person travels from Hong Kong to Beijing by airplane? (The distance between Hong Kong and Beijing is about 2000 km). How much energy is used when Hong Kong people take a bus form Tai PO city to Central city? How much energy is used if Hong Kong people drive a car instead? (The driving distance between Tai Po city and Central city is 10Km).

Science explorer, we can visit the England website. Find ways to reduce energy usage from UK people energy using methods. Energy is very important to us. We need energy to walk and carry on any actions. We need energy to grow. We also need energy from food to survive. Without energy, we will die. All machines we use need energy. Without energy the electrical appliances in our homes won't work, the machines in factories will stop.

There are different forms of energy, e.g. light, heat, sound, wind, water, electrical kinetic, chemical and potential energy. Some form energy is primary energy and it can not renew to use, e.g. light, sound, wind, water, fossil fuel etc. Some form energy is secondary energy and it can renew to use in possible, e.g. nuclear, electric charge battery etc. Why does human need to concern how to manufacture secondary energy? Because it is possible that our natural resource will be consumed all, thus we will face primary energy shortage risk. If human can invent any new form of man-made secondary energy to renew to use in order to avoid primary energy shortage to supply to use to use, then human won't only depend on our Earth natural resource energy supply numbers. We can invent any new secondary energy to renew to use again either replaces primary energy or instead of primary energy limit number supply.

What is energy change? For television energy change power case. Firstly, electrical energy changes to television power to be used by television itself, then it changes to light power, next it changes to light power. How to choose fuel form to use? Due to energy can change to different form of powers to supply different form of power advantages to supply to human to use, so it is possible that we can also invent any secondary man made renew used energy to change different form powers to supply us to use, e.g. nuclear energy changes to light or sound or heat form of powers ; electrical charge batteries changes to light or sound or heat form powers to satisfy our daily life needs.

For primary natural resource fuel energy example, different fuel has different feature, e.g. easy to burn, safe to use, gives out a lot of energy, inexpensive, produces little air pollution, easy to transport and store. How can we use in different channels, such as heating food, hot pat, driving vehicles.

For example, although coal is not expensive to cause electricity energy for past transportation tool, e.g. traditional coal energy train or our daily home cooking, but it has negative influence to environment air pollution. Hence, we ought to follow the primary natural resource energy's feature to decide how to apply what aspects of our life needs.

For example, if the country's people hope to reduce pollution when who use any kind of energy, e.g. US , Europe energy markets. The energy entrepreneur ought concentrate on manufacturing the kind of energy which can reduce environment pollution to be the least level to supply the country people to use, e.g. electric charge battery supplies to these countries' drivers to drive their vehicles on the roads, wind energy or water energy to manufacture electricity power supply to reduce air or water pollution ; or if the country people hope to buy the inexpensive energy to use, even the energy's quality and performance is worse, e.g. China, India, Hong Kong markets. The energy entrepreneur ought concentrate on manufacturing the lowest cost and enough supply of natural resource to manufacture the kind of energy to sell cheap price to these countries to use, e.g. China, Africa can accept to use e.g. gas, coal, fuel energy to use to compare developed countries people, e.g. UK, US; or if the countries people who hope to use energy which can easy to transport and store, e.g. light coal. The energy entrepreneur can choose to concentrate on manufacturing much coal to supply to the countries people to use, e.g. China, Arica Thus, to choose to manufacture which kinds of energy supply to the countries market people to use, the energy entrepreneur how decides to manufacture which kind of energy, it depends on which kinds of fuel advantages of the countries people most concerning.

How climate change raises secondary energy need and sale price increase ?

Secondary energy commercial worth

What is energy meaning? It is defined a dynamic quality, it is a fundamental entity of nature that is transferred between parts of a system in the production of physical change within the system, and it is usually regarded as the capacity for doing work, and it is usable power (such as heat or electricity) or the resources for producing such power.

Why does secondary energy own investment worth? Because the different forms of primary natural resource energy will have supply shortage crisis, such as natural resources coal, gas, solar, wind, water, geothermal, biomass(organic material) etc. However, human can attempt to explore any undiscovered Earth or Space resource to manufacture any kinds of secondary energies, e.g. nuclear energy, electric recharge battery energy to supply to electric vehicle or space robots transportation tools to use or satisfy our daily life needs in future one day. So any kind of undiscovered secondary man-made renewed used energy resources have potential commercial worth to any energy entrepreneurs, it is possible that they can replace traditional primary energy to supply to human to use for our different aspects of life needs. In the future, the secondary energy demand will increase, when primary energy supply number has decreased form natural exploration. So, it will cause the effect of any demand of secondary energy product to be raised and prices to be increased in possible. Due to global population has been growing up, considerably China and India both countries populations have been increasing rapidly. Scientists predict there are more than 1.2 billion people worldwide will lack access to electricity, and more than 2.5 billion still use wood, charcoal to cook and heat in the future when primary energy has no enough number to supply to us to use. Hence, the fact that demand is this much greater than supply to make energy a prime market for further growth.

● Energy investment risks

Although, secondary energy will have much investment worth, but energy like all other investments will carry risks. The internal and external risk factors include such as: policy is always changing to prohibit which do energy trading more easily between the energy exporting and importing countries, the secondary energy manufacturer itself own abilities to invent and to manufacture any kinds of secondary energy, improved technology can quickly make an technology obsolete, geopolitical rifts can happen overnight, the country's energy consumer (user)'s preferable choice to use which either kinds of secondary energy or secondary energy. So, it seems that (man-made) renewed used secondary energy industry can provide above-average returns, but it can also bring high risk commercial investment.

● Ways to solve energy exploration challenge

Traditionally, energy supply companies will apply those methods to operate energy providing businesses. For Shell,. Exxon examples, which had own gas stations, explore and drill for gas on their own. Other companies specialize in a part of the energy market, e.g. leasing oil rigs for example, or operating a pipeline. Energy supplying companies can choose to manufacture any kinds of energy to supply, e.g. trade oil, gas, coal, uranium, electricity etc. Any energy price and supply is demanded on the countries energy users' which kinds of energy most choice need or certain energy commodities to be chose to use popularly. For example, if US most people prefer to use secondary man-made renew used energy more than primary energy. Then, US energy manufacturers ought concentrate on manufacturing much different kinds of secondary man-made renew used energy to prepare to supply to its domestic US market in order to raise secondary energy price to sell in its country. So, the energy manufacturer's energy manufacturing choice, it is depend on which the country's people prefer to use which kinds of energy for their daily life needs.

However, scientists predict secondary energy market will have large market share, due to primary energy will have shortage to explore to supply in our earth and future energy consumers(users) prefer to choose to use more efficiency, less energy consumption, none environment pollution cause, cost effectiveness, renew to use of any kinds of energy. For example, the electricity recharge battery secondary man-made renew used energy is one kind of reducing air pollution power to push any electric battery vehicles to be driven to compare gas energy during drivers are driving their cars on the roads. They can reduce noise and air pollution and drivers can drive safely, who only need to buy one electric recharge battery to recharge in any electric recharge battery stations on streets when the electric recharge battery has no enough power to push their cars and they need to recharge their electric recharge battery drive when they had driven between one to two days. Due to primary energy, e.g. fuel , gas, the kinds of primary energies will have shortage to supply to global drivers to drive their traditional cars. Thus, the electric recharge battery or any undiscovered secondary energy will be future driving market needs. So, man-made renew used secondary energy, e.g. biofuel, hydro-electric, nuclear, will be one kind of efficient, clean, less pollution cause, cost-effective of energy to supply to our global vehicle market, even any other undiscovered new markets. Supposing they are popular to be used for electric vehicle market globally in future one day, then their prices will be decreased and constructed to average car requires up to 1,700 gallons of oil. Also supposing that making average computer requires more than ten times or weight to fossil fuels, every calories of food eaten in the US requires roughly then calories of fossil fuels. Hence, cheap energy will be one successful factor to influence future potential energy consumer (user) individual choice needs. Conversely, ion good economic times, people are more willing to travel, to buy products, and all of which success demand and low process for energy.

● Food production secondary energy need

In the future, secondary energy will be the best choice to food production market. The modern food production system is essentially a success of changing fossil fuels into food. So, raising energy prices are almost higher food costs and even shortage for fossil fuels energy. If one day, one kind of discovered secondary man-made renew used energy can supply to any restaurants or homes to be used to cook at the cheap price, then the profit is very high for this kind of food production energy. Thus, future food production secondary energy consumption market is large and because the primary energy inputs for agriculture are higher than the energy outputs of the food. However, future secondary man-made renew used energy for food production system is only one part of whole energy consumer in food industry. The food production is related to whole food consumption market which includes: household cooking energy market, agriculture or vegetable, rice, fruit etc. foods farming machines energy market, food manufacturing factories market, food machine package market, transportation food delivery market, supermarket or fruit/food sale stores market. They must need any energy inputs to achieve the food production or food transportation or warehouse / stores electricity supply or cooking energy needs. Hence, these food suppliers relate to any whole food factory manufacturers, food retailers, food wholesalers, farmers and home/restaurant cookers, all of them must need to use energy to carry on their food producing or food cooking or food transportation activities every day in overall food industry. Thus, it seems that undiscovered any second energy demand will be increased, when the primary energy supply number is decreasing. Also, when people can accept to use secondary energy to replace primary energy to be used for any cooking, transporting food, manufacturing food, food retail stores or warehouse food delivery energy need activities. Then, the secondary energy price will be fall down to attract many food energy consumers.

Nowadays, the food industry energy may includes primary nature resource gas energy or electricity energy for house house families or restaurants cooking needs, food delivering lorry drivers driving needs usually. If future second man made renew used energy is invented successful popular to be used, e.g. hydrogen, electric recharged battery energy for electric vehicles or restaurant/home families cooking needs or food factories machine maufacturing energy needs. Then, the seconday energy will have possible to replace primary energy to be food industry energy market.

Wiley, composition services graphics indicated that global primary energy consumption had been increasing 30 billion tons from 1830 year to 510 billion tons in 2010 year as well as global population size had been increasing from 70 billion 1830 yeat to 510 billion in 2010 year. Thus, it seems that global primary energy consumption will be needed largely after 2010 year. If future global nature resource primary energy is explored full number and it had not enough energy number to supply global human to use. Then, it will being many people feel uncomfortable and inconvenient,e.g. Some countries won't have enough energy to supply transportion tools to be driven, some homes and restaurants won't have enough energy to supply to cook to eat or to provide restaurant clients to eat etc. daily activies, due to human's much activities which are needs energy supply. Thus, it seems that global primary energy comsumption will be needed largely after 2010 year.

Wiley, composition services graphics also explianed that why the primary energy consumption demand can be needed to achieve the same level to the global population size increasing in 2010 year. The graph showed these reasons why cause the same level of global population size and global primary energy consumpion demand which may include: The graph showed that after a nation is developed, its per-person energy use hegins to level off. In North Ameruca and Europe, where energy demand has remained flat, or fallen dightly, in each of the past few years. But the 1.3 billion people on those two continents are far outweighted by the 5 billion people in Asia and Africa, e.g. Chinese and Indian. who currently have more energy need to comapre average per man to North America and Europe per man, ensuring

that overall energy demand will rise for years to come.
Wiley, composition services graphics also predicted that the growth in primary energy demand. China will have 4,500 million tons in 2035 year. India will have 3,000 million tons in 2035 year. Other developing Asia will have 2,000 million tons in 2035 year. Russia will have 1,500 million tons in 2035, Middle East will have 1,300 million tons in 2035, other rest of world will have 1,000 million tons in 2035. Hence, it implied that China will be the largest primary energy need country in the future.
China will be future the primary potential energy consumer market. The primary energy includes water, coal, wind, fossil oil, gas ,solar, geothermal energy, biomass (organiz material) etc. different natural resource primary energy. Otherwise, US, UK, Europe will be secondary energy potential need market. For example, electrical recharge battery energy will be raised demand to supply to any future new design electrical charge battery vehicles in US, Europe, UK markets.
Due to US, Europe, UK people concern environment protection, so they will invent many electric charge battery vehicles to consume electrical charge battery to replace polluted gas energy to avoid air pollution when the drivers are driving cars on themselve countries' roads. For example, second man-made renew used nuclear energy can be applied to rockets to pusch them to leave our earth to fly to other space far away and consuming nuclear energy will be cost efficient, and nuclear energy saving will be more when nuclear to spend long time to be used in any long time space journey. Hence, nuclear energy and electric charge battery secondary energy will be popular to be applied to vehicles and rockets energy needs in US, Europe, potential marketss, even our daily energy needs in global second energy market.

- Law and policies in engery supply industry

Every energy entrepreneur needs to consider how whose government implement law and policies to prohibit whose energy consumption, energy distribution and energy production behavior in order to protect energy consumers can have fair price energy purchase from the country's energy suppliers between themselves. For US energy law and policy example, the energy independence and security Act of 2007 year. It's major provisions include: Accelerated research of clean energy technologies Act, energy savings in building and industry Act, improved standards for appliances and lighting Act, improved vehical fuel economy Act and increased production of biofuel Act. It aims to prohibit any US energy manufacturing suppliers do any unfair energy trading transaction behavior to its domestic or foreign energy consumers immortally.

● Energy entrepreneur's business strategy

Before you decide to operate either any kinds of secondary energy or primary energy supply business or both kinds of energy supply business. I recommend that you need to consider how to solve these questions before choosing which kind of energy product to manufacture. The questions may include as below:

Who are your energy business's competitors (peers)? How do they compare? How have your energy business company performed cyclically? How to choose to manufacture to sell which kinds of primary or secondary energy product(s), either manufactures only primary energy product(s) or manufactures only secondary energy products or both? Which countries do you plan to sell your energy product?

Illustration by Wilsey, composition services graphiss showed that these natural resources to energy product the world's electricity percentage, such as below:

41% of coal, 5% of oil, 21% of gas, 13% of nuclear, 16% of Hydro, 3% other renewable secondary man-made energy.

Hence, coal will be future the major natural resource to produce electricity. The energy entrepreneur ought attempt to explore any coal resources, when who choose to supply electricity power to consumers for future energy consumption country markets.

Wiley, composition services also predicted that the expectation is that North America coal will supply the expectation is that North America coal will supply Asian demand, Us export terminals have a total capacity of 173 million tommes output. China will drive 16% of the nations total output. China will drive the sea-born demand for coal over for the forcessable future. Chinese energy consumption will grow more than 12 % between 1980 and 2009 years. Though, China heads global demand, India is growing faster in terms of coal imports. Much of the global coal demand will be supplied by Indonesia and Australia. Colombia, Russia, South Africa and Mongolia are also players in global export coal energy resources.

Consequently, I believe that secondary energy will be one kind of new energy product to replace traditional primary energy product for human energy consumption market global needs. Hence, it is right time any energy entrepreneur needs to research how to explore any undiscovered man-made renew used secondary energy products to avoid primary energy shortage crisis occurrence.

How climate change influences migrant decision to bring economy influence ?
How and why climate change influence migrant right change ? When migrant right change, how it influence migrant immigrating desire ? The interlinkages between climate change and human rights are deep and complex, with climate change impacting a wide range of internationally protected human rights; such as rights to health and even life and rights to food, water, shelter and property. In this paper, I am going to discuss the effect of climate change on protected human rights relating to migration, focusing primarily on the relationship between international refugee law and climate change.
There remains uncertainty on how severe global warming will be and its precise impacts on society, but there is a 97 per cent consensus among experts that a rapid build-up of greenhouse gas is due to human activities.The Earth's climate is gradually changing due to the continuous concentration of anthropogenic greenhouse gas (GHG) emissions into the atmosphere. The Earth's surface temperature is getting warmer at a disturbing rate, and has become significantly warmer in the last 150 years after 10,000 years of relative stability.[3] Most climate change projections are based on a two-degree Celsius increase in global mean temperature from the temperature in 1850, which has now been agreed by most States as the threshold for 'dangerous' climate change.
The consequences of climate change are more obvious now due to the increased prevalence of rising sea levels, extreme weather conditions, drought and desertification, and these consequences will have significant effects on the ecosystem, specifically on food security, migration, and health. The political, economic, and social capacity of a country, which includes its infrastructure, economic stability, and ability to help its population when in need, will affect individual's ability to cope with the impacts of climate change, and therefore the impacts will be felt differently in different communities. In the 1980s and 1990s, climate change was primarily viewed as an environmental and scientific issue, but in 1990 the potential impacts of climate change on human migration were identified by the Intergovernmental Panel on Climate Change (IPCC). The IPCC stated that millions of people would likely be uprooted by shoreline erosion, coastal flooding, and agricultural disturbances (such as salination of crops),and that climate change might require consideration of 'migration and resettlement outside of national boundaries.

However, the relationship between climate change and forced migration has emerged as one of the most studied, but contested, fields of inquiry, and the lack of agreement on the links between climate change and forced migration explains why the call for the recognition of so-called 'climate change refugees' has been unsuccessful. Legally, there is no such thing as a 'climate change refugee,' and this point will be expanded upon later in this paper, but there is, however, evidence that people are moving in response to the effects of climate change. Cross-border displacement resulting from natural disasters and the effects of climate change has therefore been identified as a normative gap in the international legal protection regime.Determining how exactly climate change affects people's decisions to move is crucial in determining how appropriate the call for the inclusion of people displaced by gradual or sudden environmental impacts within the refugee protection framework.

As discussed above, there is an ongoing debate and scepticism as to the direct link between climate change and displacement, but there is now mounting evidence which supports the plight of so-called 'climate change refugees' and demands attention from the international legal community. The term 'climate change refugee' is often used to describe those who will be forced to leave their homes because of climate change impacts. In this section, I will focus on the extent to which international refugee law may apply, and discuss why, by and large, it is an inappropriate framework for responding to the needs of the displaced.

The first official use of the term 'climate change refugee' was by Essam El-Hinnawi in a United Nations Environment Programme (UNEP) report, where he described people who are forced to leave their places of residence because of human or naturally induced environmental issues as 'environmental refugees'. El-Hinnawi was not trying to make a legal argument for the extension of refugee law to cover those displaced for environmental reasons, but instead was using the term to highlight the potentially devastating effects of unchecked development and pollution. Since then the term has been used in almost any discussion involving the impacts of climate change and forced migration. While those displaced internally (within their own countries) can be protected using the United Nations Guiding Principles on Internal Displacement mechanism, or even by the national law of their own countries, those displaced by environmental impacts and who are crossing or wish to cross their countries' borders currently have no legal basis for this type of movement in international law.

The relationship between climate change, natural disasters, and migration

What is the positive or negative impacts when climate change causes disasters and then bring migration number increases or decreases? The relationship between climatic shocks, natural disasters, and migration has received increasing attention in recent years and is quite controversial. One view suggests that climate change and its associated natural disasters increase migration. An alternative view suggests that climate change may only have marginal effects on migration. Knowing whether climate change and natural disasters lead to more migration is crucial to better understand the different channels of transmission between climatic shocks and migration and to formulate evidence-based policy recommendations for the efficient management of the consequences of disasters.

What are the positive and negative impacts when climate change causes natural disasters and migration attributes? I shall indicate as below:

On migration benefit aspect, it may include these such as: migration can help people cope with the adverse effects of climatic shocks by providing them with new opportunities and resources. Remittances from overseas migrants increase after disasters in their home countries and play an important role in mitigating the adverse effects of climatic shocks and natural disasters. Climatic factors, such as natural disasters or rainfall and temperature variations, may increase international migration through their effect on internal migration. Agricultural productivity represents one of the pathways that can explain the relationship between climatic shocks and migration.

However, climate change may also bring these disadvantages on migration benefit aspect, they may include such as: Public intervention both before and after disasters helps build resilience and can explain why migration responses differ according to different shocks. The migration response to disasters depends on the nature of the shock (slow vs rapid onset events), its severity, and the vulnerability of the affected people.Due to liquidity constraints, poor people might not be able to migrate in the aftermath of climatic shocks. Also, in developing countries, international migration due to disasters may be driven by highly educated people, which may foster brain drain in a vulnerable context.

Climate Change and the Migrant Crisis

What is climate change and migrant crisis ? It may include as below:

For India example, when climate change , it can influence India migrant decision. India has the first airport which is solely functioning on solar energy. The world can learn from India or China. The West has to stop dumping subsidized agar products into third world destroying local agar industry and pushing people into poverty. Western fisheries are just taking all fish from coasts of Africa. If these policies continue, europeans dont complain people coming to your countries. For afria example, Africa has tripled their population from 400 million to over 1.2 billion people in the past 40 years. Overpopulation, not climate change is their root problem. Africa now has 1 and quarter billion Africans living in some of the world's wort market places. This new lie (scheme) is a dreamed up scheme to import as many as they can into the first world market places, Europe, u.s., Australia, place them on welfare, make the tax payers foot the bill for all the goods and services they can consume to maximize annualized corporate profits making, and to turn them into citizens and have the tax payers pay to educate them so hopefully they will in the future expand taxes uptake for the government's. All paid for by the tax payers. you get to be absorbed genetically. So, it seems that climate change will bring more negative impact to migrants , when the country can attract many migrants choose to emigrate to the county to live, due to climate change infuences.

● Vulnerable countries number will increase when climate change become worse to influence human live as well as human needs to learn new skills to adapt difficult lives

The relationship between migration and the environment is not new. From the mid-19th century Great Irish Famine to the early 20th century Dust Bowl, we have many examples in history of people choosing or being forced to migrate because of changes in their physical environments. What is new now is that the world is grappling with the devastating impacts of climate change. With greater awareness came increased political recognition and there is now a widespread consensus on the need to address the adverse impacts of climate change on the migration of people now and in the future.

Climate migration is a reality in all parts of the world, however, the situation in what is known as "vulnerable countries" represents a particular challenge. Vulnerable countries are Least Developed Countries (LDCs), Landlocked Developing Countries (LLDCs) and Small Island Developing States (SIDS). In 2016, the 15 countries with the highest vulnerability to natural hazards were LDCs, LLDCs and SIDS. These countries are disproportionately affected by the negative impacts of climate change and are often least able to cope due to their structural constraints and geographical disadvantages. At the same time, they contribute the least to climate change. These countries are among the strongest advocates for more robust action on climate migration as they face very real challenges that affect all aspects of the daily lives of their populations.

Climate migration challenges take multiple forms in these vulnerable countries. In LDCs, the poorest and most vulnerable segment of the international community, climate change pressures can intersect with numerous development-related challenges as well as security issues. The combination of those factors often leads people to migrate in search of better or safer lives. For example, the Lake Chad Basin is currently experiencing grave environmental degradation, in a context where populations face the violence linked to the presence of groups such as Boko Haram. Migration patterns in that region have been reshaped due to these factors. Some LDCs such as Ethiopia and Bangladesh are sometimes saddled with the "double stress" of having to deal with internal climate migration, while also hosting large numbers of refugees from neighboring countries. LLDCs often have scarce water resources, further depleted by the impacts of climate change. This can create pressure on populations to migrate for better access to water. For example, nomadic pastoralists are often pushed to alter their traditional routes and travel further and for longer periods in search of water and land resources. Climate change is also affecting livelihoods, such as in Mongolia where extremely cold winters called dzud deplete nomadic livestock and destroy agriculture opportunities, pushing rural populations to migrate to urban centers.

SIDS are recognized as a special case for sustainable development as they face greater risk of marginalization due to their small size and remoteness. They also have fragile natural environments, and natural disasters such as storms and cyclones have a devastating impact on the population. The adverse impacts of climate change have contributed to the migration of thousands of people in SIDS in the last decade alone. One specific type of migration in this context is the planned relocation of people, where entire communities need to be moved, generally further inland, to escape climate change impacts such as coastal erosion. In Fiji, following Tropical Cyclone Winston in 2016, more than 60 villages were relocated to reduce people's exposure and vulnerability to further risks.

The current situation is clearly preoccupying and addressing the negative impacts of climate change on the migration of people in vulnerable countries should represent a priority now and for the future. We are moving towards a high level week of crucial political dialogues at the United Nations General Assembly in September 2019. In particular, the United Nations Climate Action Summit is a key opportunity to highlight the challenges of most vulnerable countries and put forward commitments and solutions to address climate migration issues.

On conclusion, riority should be given to mitigate the impacts of climate change and promote climate change adaptation in places where populations are at risk of forced migration. However, it is also clear that in some places, it will not be possible for populations to remain in situ and it is of utmost importance to think about how legal migration options can be offered to those migrants. It is also important to factor in the positive role that migrants can play in the fight against climate change, such as by facilitating remittances and transfer of skills and knowledge towards climate action. So, climate change influences human needs to change skills to adapt difficult lives.

How climate change impacts on developing countries economy ?

In fact, climate change will increase global temperature change rainfall patterns and will result in more frequent and severe floods and drought. Depending on future emission of greenhouse gases, global temperatures are likely to rise between 2 degree and 4 degree within the next century. The main impacts of climate change will however not be felt through higher temperatures, but through a change in the hydrological cycle. Rainfall is likely to increase around the poles and the tropics when in the sub-tropics average precipitation is likely to decrease. Not only the average annual or seasonal rainfall will change, there also be an increase in the number of extreme events resulting in most frequent and severe floods and droughts.

How does climate change influence to development countries? Climate change will influence any development countries on these several aspects. They include as below:

On trade influence hand, reducing emission levels from the developing world is extremely important. If current developments are continuing, for example, emissions from China and India both countries will save be much higher than the total emission form all Europe countries. Currently, the Europe is stimulating mitigation and transfer of clean technologies through the clean development mechanism (CDM). Although, it is still unclear what the mitigation potential of the (CDM) is, especially in India the investment is (CDM) projects is significant. However, the Europe should take a much wider approach. In developing countries a lot can be done in terms of increasing energy efficiency, land use change and agriculture. It is also important that developing countries are stimulated to choose a sustainable, low emission developed pathway. Choices for more sustainable, low emission technologies should be made early in the process. It seems that climate changing will encourage many countries will choose to do more environment protection related trading, e.g. researching how to invent environment protection new products to reduce our earth pollution between European and any developing countries, such as China and India etc.

On focus mitigation efforts in least developed countries on land use change, agriculture development aspect, in the least developed countries mitigation efforts should not focus on the energy or transport sector, but on agriculture and forestry. Agriculture is responsible for a relatively large percentage of the emissions in many developing countries, e.g. Africa, China, Malaysia, Hong Kong, Japan etc. In this sector there are many win options both reducing poverty and reducing greenhouse gas emissions. For example, improved water and nutrient management can sharply increase production efficiency and reduces at least the amount of emission per kg food produced. Agro-forestry reduces greenhouse gas emission through increased carbon storage and reduces poverty through diversifying the incomes of local communities.

However, in most developing countries, the main limitation in coping with the impacts of climate change is a lack of capacity. Besides a lack of capacity, in many developing countries, there is also a significant lack of data and knowledge on climate change impacts. Developing countries should be stimulated to improve data gathering and make existing data more easily available.However, no migration effort will stop the need for adaptation. Especially, the least developed countries, who have contributed little to the problem will suffer the most.

On business strategies for climate change aspect, nowadays, the valuation for clean-technology companies, have increased considerable and the corporate carbon footprint has become an important topic to be discussed how to solve among senior managers? How can firms profit from what they do to address climate change? Thus, a low-carbon economy is already especially in energy, transport and heavy industry.

If current climate science holds true and there is considerable uncertainty in the estimates, global greenhouse gas emissions should ideally decrease from today's levels by 90 percent as of 2050 year in order to certain global warming below two degrees centigrade. Hence, it seems global warmth challenge brings further any new energy potential development businesses. Due to environment scientists encourage us to be realized the necessary increase in carbon productivity and new low-carbon technologies that are necessary dramatically reduces energy consumption and direct greenhouse gas emissions will have to be developed and then implemented widely to avoid future serious global environment warmth caused climate changes and pollution challenges occurrence.

Reference

Hugo, G. (199). Environmental concerns and
International migration. International migration
Review., 30. Pp. 105-131.

Mendelsohn , R., (2013) " Climate Change And Economic Growth Commission On Growth And Development" working paper no 60.

Stern, N., (ed.) The economics of climate change: The Stern Review, Cambridge University Press, Cambridge, 2006, p.3.

Stern, N. (2007). The Economics Of Climate Change:
The Stern Review, Cambridge UK:
University Press.

UNHCR/WFP (United Nations High Commission For Refugees) World Food Program, 2009. Acute Malnutrition in protected refugee situation: A global strategy Geneva: UNHCR/WFP.

Zarocostas , J. 2011. Famine and disease threaten millions in drought hit horn of Africa. BMJ 343: doi: 10,1136/bmj.d4a4a <online 21 July 2011>.

CHAPTER NINE

Reason the transport supply and Tesco stores fresh sale cooperation may raise sale price

● This case concerns chain involved in the supply of fresh fruit and vegetables to Tesco stores cooperation challenge

The place(P) of the traditional marketing mix decides about channel intermediaries or middlemen to use an outdated, yet user friendly, term and the management of physical distribution. Placing products involves managing the process supporting the flow of goods or services from producers to consumers.

The process has sometimes been described as developing the best routes to market for a firm's products. Products must be made available in the right quantity, in the right location, and at the times when customers wish to purchase them. Marketing channels can perform an important role in the later stages of a value chain, in particular outbound logistic (e.g. order processing, storage and transportation); marketing and sales (e.g. market research, personal selling, sales promotion) and after sales service. However, it depends on which kinds of business to need outbound logistic, such as Tesco supermarket only needs ordering fresh fruit and vegetables from local farmers, then these foods need to be stored in refrigerate in warehouse and transport these foods to different supermarkets by vans. So, Tesco value chain only needs outbound logistic activity, but it does not need marketing and sales and after sale service to sell its fresh fruit and vegetables to its clients from its supermarkets (stores). In fact, Tesco stores

is such UK farmer's intermediaries which can add value by breaking bulk. This might involve purchasing in large quantities of fruits and vegetables from UK local farmers and then selling smaller, more manageable, to keep volumes of fresh food stock in warehouses, then its vans will deliver these fresh fruits and vegetables to different stores daily. Discrepancies of fruit foods quantity are reduced by Tesco (intermediary) who provides every store clients with individual preferable fresh foods items that suit their needs daily. Tesco stores can offer superior knowledge of a target market compared with farmers, for example by ensuring which kinds of vegetables or fruits foods numbers are stocked in every store to match the economic and lifestyle needs of Tesco store shoppers who live in the area. Probably the most important gaps between Tesco store shoppers and UK local farmers in channel management are indicated at those of location and time. A location gap occurs owing to the geographic separation of farmers and the store shoppers of their fresh fruit and vegetables foods. UK farmers generally want to grow their fruits and vegetable food in one central location (farming), but farmers' food buyers typically want to buy their growing foods locally. A time gap arises when the UK local farmers' fresh foods buyers want to buy whose fresh growing foods at a time when a UK local farmer may considerate it inconvenient to make the available. UK local farmers may like to grow fresh fruits and vegetable foods at night from 8:00 PM to 12:00PM, then who will collect these fresh foods
from 5:00 AM to 7:00 in the morning, but their buyers may want to buy in the evenings or at weekends afternoon. Tesco stores (intermediary) need to facilitate vans to transport these fresh fruits and vegetables foods from farmers' farming to its one central warehouse to deliver to different stores to sell the budget numbers of different kinds of foods to every local store consumers more exactly (Adrian, P. 2012).

Tesco stores is one of the world's largest retailers, it has social responsibility to protect fresh fruit and vegetable to sell to clients. It had attempted to predict customer behavior about hope much fresh fruit and vegetable and what kinds of fresh fruit and vegetable whose consumers will buy from data statistic in warehouse. It aims to reduce excess fruit and vegetable stocks in warehouse to cause perishable. In the winter might have seen choice reduced to basic items such as potatoes, cabbage, apples, supplemented by canned fruit and vegetables. Look in a Tesco supermarket today, and clients may find difficult to tell the season of the year or the distance from the countryside, simple based on the fruit and vegetables with are on display. In UK supermarket sector is intensely competitive, and has seen continuous innovation in the way it seeks to satisfy customers' needs. As consumers have become wealthier, the supermarkets realized that buyers would no longer be content with the staple foods such as cabbage and potatoes in the depths of winter-significant numbers of them now wanted excitement on a plate, and all year round. Furthermore, if they were planning a menu, they wanted to be sure that when they went to their local supermarket.

By and large, supermarkets have been key drivers of the value for the groceries that they sell. They have been close to their customers and identified their changing needs. They have built confidence with their customers, who can trust freshness and provenance of food they sell and the reliability of supply. It is therefore the supermarkets who have gone seeking sources of supply, rather than growers aggressively seeking to sell the produce that they have available. Before, the development of very large supermarket chains, retailers were more
fragmented. They did not have the power or resources to innovate with new product lines which they could then commission a grower to produce. Today, supermarket such as Tesco invest heavily in their food technology laboratories, and can then go to suppliers and place large orders with exacting standards with regard to price, quality, and delivery. Above all else, supermarkets have put themselves at the center of a slick distribution system which connects an international networks of growers through transport networks of trucks, ships and planes to put fresh produce in their network of stores, every day, all year around. The efficiency of the logistics, and the bargaining power of the supermarkets has often led to the price being charged at a British supermarket being lower than the price changed in supermarkets thousands of miles away where fruit and vegetables were grown. Tomatoes grown in Bulgaria and sold in Britain can be cheaper in Britain in local Bulgarian shops. The bizarre situation has occurred where the supermarkets import apples from France to be sold in Kent, the traditional home of British apple growing, plums from Poland to be sold in the grown product in Lincolnshire. Supermarkets argue that sourcing from overseas is not just an issue of cost saving more importantly, the supermarkets seek a continuity of supplies from large growers who can guarantee to deliver a specified quantity at a specified quantity at a specified time and place. The supermarkets capable of achieving this. British supermarkets are among the most efficient in the world, and their desire

to ensure that customers can always get what they want may explain the mass transport of food. Local farmers' market may could environmentally friendly, but they rarely guarantee a continuity of supplies. As part of their drive for efficiency, supermarkets have a tendency to move food , such potatoes could being transported several hundred miles between distribution centers before they end up on a supermarket shelf just a few miles from where potatoes were grown. The environmental campaigning group Sustain has estimated that the average children travels 2,000 between the farm where it was grown and the supermarket shelf and furthermore the distance products travel from farm to end customer increased by an estimated 25 per cent between 1980 year and 2007 year (Priesnitz 2007).

Global warming had become an important issue with many clients and there was growing concern that supermarkets' practice of transporting fresh produce long distances around the world was irresponsibly adding to greenhouse gas emissions. Hence, distance travelled was one of value chain factor Terso supermarket needs to consider their fruit and vegetables food to keep fresh in refrigerate to transport to retailers to sell in UK. The most contentious food miles are clocked up by fresh fruit and vegetables flow in by plane from overseas. Although, air freighted produce accounted for less than 1 per cent of total UK food miles, it was the fastest growing way of moving foods around. One response By Tesco was to introduce a greatest proportion of local produce. To achieve this, it placed buyers and marketing teams in the regions in order to get a clear picture of local markets and to develop relationships with suppliers. By 2007 year, Tesco claimed to have 7,000 regional lines from throughout the UK, which were promoted as local produce, supporting local growers and reducing greenhouse gas emissions. Throughout its history, Tesco has demonstrated its ability to listen to what customers want, and this has been true in respect of its distribution system. The weaknesses of commodity systems are particularly for major customers, such as Mc Donalds, commodity systems do not lead to reliability in supply, quality, quantity or price nor high rates of innovation on which they can differentiate their offer from their competitors. The opportunity and challenge of fresh food product differentiation, so Tesco stores need to innovation to give rise to a number of strategic options to keep vegetables and fruits to be fresh in the short time to sell full numbers. If a firm, such as Tesco is the lowest cost producer than commodity market strategy can be an attractive strategic option. As Tesco stores fresh food sale that it's larger competitors shall find difficult to copy. Otherwise, Smaller size stores can sometimes be a competitive advantage.

Tesco stores (fresh food retailer) need to co-operate with suppliers and fresh food growers to align the whole chain to the changing needs of consumers. The food chain strategy aims to deliver superior value to specific groups of customers. Tesco stores work closely with its fresh food suppliers to develop specific products for each range. Both the supplier and growers understand the Tesco marketing strategy and their role in the innovation process. Tesco is actively seeking new chain ideas and is prepared to pay for such efforts. From a primary producer and supplier perspective the range of brands enables Tesco to work with suppliers to market the total crop .

Chapter 10 Reasons of societal marketing orientation may help body shop to raise sale price

What is the difference between production orientation and societal marketing orientation and sales orientation to body shop ?

Critically assess the extent to which whether Body Shop to be a truly marketing oriented organization throughout its 30 years history.The body shop international power line carrier (the body shop) was founded by Dame Anita Roddick in the England in 1976. It sold personal beauty care products, such as baby and child specific products, bath and shower and colour cosmetics, deodorants, skin care, hair care, fragrances, sun care etc skin health products to provide human body benefits. Nowadays, the body shop was skin and body care manufacturer and retailer operating in 55 countries with over 2,100 stores. It had 42 exclusive outlets in Hong Kong. It's missions were to dedicate to pursuit of social and environment change to meaningfully contribute to local, national and international communities in which trade to passionately campaign for the protection of the environment, human and civil rights and against animal testing and to make fun, passion and care part of our daily lives (Adrian, P. 2012).

There are five main marketing orientations of which a company will adopt one. This will determine the way it interacts with the customer. Such as product orientation suggests that a company focuses inwards looking at what it is capable of, rather than the needs and wants of the client; sales orientation is based upon selling existing products with a turnover sale numbers relationship marketing orientation recognizes the value of repeat business over, not only with customers but suppliers as well; societal marketing orientation is relatively new in the scheme of things but suggests on top of meeting the needs and wants of the customer and the organization there is the societies interests to be looked and marketing orientation is based around the needs and wants of a customer to meet business objectives and it assumes that a sale depends on a customer's decision to purchase a product or provide a service.

● What is marketing two levels meaning ?

Marketing can be seen at two levels, the first level is such as a business philosophy, marketing puts customers at the center of an organization's consideration and which is reflected in basic values , such as the requirement to understand and respond to customers' needs and the necessary to search constantly for new market opportunity. In a truly marketing oriented organization, these values are instilled in all employees and should influence their behavior without any need for prompting. The personnel manager would have a selection policy that recruited staff who could fulfil the needs of customers rather than simply minimizing the wage bill in any marketing oriented organization. The other level is techniques of marketing also include pricing, the design of channels of distribution and new product development.

● What are the three components of market orientation ?

The assessing the nature and importance of market orientation for large firms, such as body shop. The three components of market orientation could be analytically separated. The components of market orientation organization include the first component is the customer orientation, it means an organization must have a thorough understanding of its target buyers, so that it can create a product of superior value to give client benefits ; the second component is the competitor orientation, it means any firm should look at how well its competitors are able to satisfy buyers' needs. It should understand the short term strengths and weaknesses and long term capabilities and strategies of current and potential competitors as well as the third component is to develop marketing plans that are not acted upon by people who are capable of delivering promises made to customers and a marketing orientation organization requires that the organization draws upon and integrates its human and physical resources effectively and adapts them to meet client's needs. Otherwise, a production and sales orientation may be appropriate to firms at certain stages in the evolution of markets. Where the dominant business environment is based on the need for good production planning above all, the company that does this best will achieve the greatest overall business success.

It is either production orientation, it means organizations that produce what they imagined consumers wanted, rather than what they actually wanted. Planning for full utilization of capital equipment are often seen as more important than ensuring that equipment is used to provide goods and services that people actually wants. Production-oriented firms generally aim for efficiency in production rather than effectiveness in meeting customer's needs . It is either or selling orientation, it means advertising, sales promotion and personal selling techniques are used to emphasize product differentiation and brands and it does not focus on satisfying client needs or desire new product offerings and production led. Hence, one market orientation organization needs to focus on satisfying clients' needs profitably by these marketing mix, such as product, price, place, physical evidence, processed, people and promotion. Anyway ,Market orientation implied that body shop , which ought seek information about clients, such as current and future needs and took action based this information (client orientation); it ought seek information about competitors' current strengths and weaknesses and their long term strategies and took actions based on these information (competitor orientation) ; it ought coordinate the actions taken by sharing clients and competitors information internally (intra-firm communication).

● What is the three components of market orientation ?

The three components of market orientation meant social marketing and understanding boarder concerns and ethical environmental, legal and social context of marketing activities and programs. The cause and effects of marketing clearly beyond the company and the consumer to society as whole. New terms humanistic marketing and ecological marketing were suggested to societal marketing concept.

● What is the social marketing concept ?

The social marketing concept holds that the organization's task is to determine the needs, wants and interests of target markets and to deliver the desired satisfactions more effectively and
efficiently than competitors and the society's welling being, such as body shop had achieved sales and profit gains by adopting and practicing a form of the societal marketing concept called cause related marketing.

● DISCUSSION

Body Shop is marketing orientation organization in 30 years.Critically assess the extent to which I consider Body Shop to be a truly marketing oriented organization throughout its 30 years history . It seemed body shop had achieved cause-related marketing as an opportunity to enhance their corporate reputation, raised brand awareness, increased customer loyalty and built sales. It's corporate values were composed of five core values. The first one was to oppose animal testing. The opposing animal testing for both cosmetic products and ingredients began in 1976 years.

In the 1980 year and 1990 year, who successfully campaigned with animal protection groups to change the UK and European laws to support the development products were tried on human volunteers. Along with the development of technology testing had played a leading role to protect the rights of both human and animals . The second one was to support community trade, it initiated the trade not aid objective of creating trade to help people in the third world utilizing their resources to their own needs. This reflects communities needed a fair price for natural ingredients who purchased from these often marginalized countries. The third one was to activate self esteem. Women were the main customers and employees in the body shop. The fourth one was to defend human rights. The body shop had long campaign on human rights, highlighting abuses and increasing the global awareness of issues by making full use of the geographic advantages of their shops and supporting other human rights organizations. The last one was protect our plant. In 2001 year, huge campaign against global warming was hosted by the body shop and green peace, who advocated the use of recyclable source and materials (Adrian, P. 2012). Although profits were an essential element of long run survival in body shop and it was likely to be overall corporate and marketing objectives, but body shop seemed more to be required level of profits rather than profit that there were many other objectives, which might pursue through its pricing strategies . For example, if body shop wanted to maximize market share or simply survive, a different set of prices would be delivered than if the objectives were to maximize profits. Hence, body shop ought to see viewpoint the marketing side of pricing and it ought not to see viewpoint the production / supply side of pricing if it was a truly marketing oriented organization.

The key inputs for body shop to make pricing decision whether it was marketing oriented or productive / supply oriented included production objectives or marketing objectives, demand or supply numbers were considered cost or sale price and competitors or clients consideration factors, such as beauty skin care products in competitive markets demand, i.e. To decide the price whether customers are willing and able to pay is a major consideration in the selection of pricing strategies and levels of demands . Hence, body shop ought to consider demand numbers , it ought not consider production / supply numbers if it was a truly marketing oriented organization. For example, since most of the body shop's factories were still located in the UK, where wages and salaries were much higher than in Asia, so UK itself sale product prices were higher than that from Asia itself sale product prices.

I think Body Shop was a truly marketing oriented organization more than production/supply oriented organization throughout its 30 years history. In fact, Body Shop was experiencing market level growth. It could expand its sales market in Europe, America, Middle East, Asia and Africa etc different countries. It seemed that it had attempted to carry on marketing research to decide to choose which countries would have more client numbers to demand to buy its personal care products, then it would follow the countries' estimated client numbers to produce its products to sell to the countries. So, it was why some Asia countries sold its bath and shower and skin and hair care and colour cosmetics products more than its fragrances products, such as Hong Kong young people were more acceptable to use bath and show and color cosmetic and skin and hair care products more than fragrances products . It seemed that Hong Kong Body Shop sold fragrance products numbers were less than bath and shower and color cosmetics etc. products. Nowadays, I think the personal beauty care products new businesses which planned to entry this market was more difficult. It was possible than Body Shop was a famous personal beauty care products sale company, it had owned many clients too many years. So , it caused barriers to any new personal beauty care product competitors felt difficult to entry this market .Furthermore, Body Shop had build strong buyer and seller power to increase clients had more confident to use its products, it was possible that who felt its different kind of products could give more health to their skin or body more than other similar personal beauty care products. Moreover, I believe Body Shop had attempted to carry on technological experimenting to aim to build different countries' clients had more confident to use its products forever.

In conclusion, it seemed that Body Shop was truly marketing oriented organization more than productive/ supply oriented organization oriented organization throughout its 30 years history.

Any companies need to consider the social responsibility during which are the pursuits of profit and meeting the needs of wider group of stakeholders incompatible. Without this self interest, there will be little motivation for firms to provide better services, workers couldn't earn better salaries and clients couldn't aspire for a high level of consumption. Hence, self interest which helps markets work more effectively for the benefits of all. Hence, companies should adopt a code of behavior and conduct and ethical behavior which would not influence any stakeholders groups' benefits to pursuit their profit honestly. Corporate social responsibility is a form of corporate self regulation integrated into a business model. It aims to give responsibility for corporate actions and to encourage a positive impact on the environment and stakeholders including consumers, employees, investors, communities and others and it is titled to aid an organization's mission as well as guide to what the company can give the best benefits to serve its customers. I shall use body shop company as one example to judge whether what extent are the pursuits of profit and meeting the needs of wider groups of stakeholders will be incompatible.

In fact, body shop could adopt a code of behavior and conduct and ethical behavior which would not influence any stakeholders groups' benefits to pursuit their profit honestly. Such as, one of the major and most successful initiatives which body shop used an effective supply chain for their products and body shop made use of their sustainable chain supply strategy to ensure that there was the promotion and the maintenance of the social ethical behavior in its business. Hence, it seemed that body shop could be compatible to achieve an effective supply chain to deliver to different countries' stores to meet clients who had more need to buy different kinds of skin care products to provide them to choose to buy in the reasonable price choices in the short time. It is therefore in the best practices and interests for body shop to reach out to the communities in their businesses to provide raw materials to help the manufacturers of the beauty products. It also partook in the development of the market for such small scale suppliers. In many cases the body shop tried to outsource its raw materials to its customers. This had ensured the sustainability of its customer base this included it's sensitivity to its environment and the required standards of the labor practices of its partners. Hence, it seemed that body shop could be compatible to help its partners to earn profits and any countries' partners could provide more job chances to unemployed people to work from body shop's outsourcing strategy.

Hence, this had been developed by the body shop by including strategies, such as third party logistic providers and intermediaries in which who had no ownership. The body shop was a multinational company also adopted trading to purchasing approach where it shifted from short term where focus of buying articles to long term focus of fewer suppliers. This was an attempt of it to develop quality products where prices were also fair and affordable to sell to different countries‘ clients. It seemed that body shop could be compatible to sell reasonable prices of products to it's clients. Moreover, it had included in its strategies the aspect of business promotion using catalogues. For the same reason, it had been involved in printing of catalogues which were given out to the clients with their purchases. It was important to note that it' catalogues always contained all it's information descriptions and any person who purchased it's products was bound to receive the explanation of all it's product. This was an attempt of it to develop quality products where prices were also fair and affordable to sell to different countries‘ clients. It seemed that body shop could be compatible to provide clear information description in catalogues to let whose clients to know what it's different kinds of style body skin care products ingredients and benefits were , then who could compare it's products to other competitors to decide to buy or not buy fairly.

In Oct. 2007 the campaign for safe cosmetic products, in which 25 multinational companies participated, tested 33 brand name lipsticks and found one-third of the sampled exceeded the limit of lead allowed in confectionery. The affected brands included L'Oreal and Christian Dior. A definite effect would be that consumers would be more concerned regarded the ingredients of products who used, which was likely to have an effect on cosmetics and skin care products were released to capture share. It seemed body shop needed to consider its beauty personal care products were the most ensure to own organic ingredients to let any countries clients (stakeholder) to meet their body health care needs (Adrian, P. 2012).

On the health and natural aspect, body shop had health and safe responsibility to consumers. Although, I felt who had considered this issue because it had 30 years history to operate this business and it had not received any serious negative complaints damage its health product image from clients before. However, with consumers were increasingly informed and were educated, who were now more demanding for more information regarding products and were becoming more aware of health issue. Products with organic ingredients and natural ingredients, such as tea and plants were gaining popular. Furthermore, consumers were looking for healthier substitutes to seemingly unhealthy products, such as color cosmetics. Hence, body shop began to sell the reducing numbers, it was possible due to clients compared it's body care products quality to the other competitors and who felt it's product's ingredients existed some poor ingredients to cause every one's body to be unhealthy.

Hence, it's productive processing was very important. It seemed that body shop could be compatible to consider its individual client body skin health issue whether after who had used it's body skin care products to have skin hurt or skin pain feeling. In conclusion, to judge what extent are the pursuits of profit and meeting the needs of wider groups of stakeholders incompatible for any individual business, it is depended on whether the company's any stakeholders, such as employees, clients, suppliers, partners, society (communities) etc. who will have positive or negative influence from it. I feel that it will be incompatible if the company give negative influence to any one of its stakeholder. Hence, if any one company's at least one stakeholder who felt who had negative influence due to it did business to relate to whom unwillingly, then it's pursuit of profits aim would be incompatible to meet it's needs of its any one of stakeholder. Such as body shop will give positive influence to its all stakeholders. Hence, I feel it is compatible extent to pursuit of profit and meeting the needs of its wider groups of stakeholders definitely.

I feel that Nestle company has managed to sustainable reconcile to pursuit profits and meeting the needs of its wider groups of stakeholders two aims compatibly. Nestle was the world's largest food and beverage company. Nestle in the United States, which represented seven operating across the USA country and it was the first expanded effort in USA and achievement tied to Nestle 's global sustainability principle and commitment. Nowadays, It served 97% of American householders and Nestle 's mission was to lead the industry in nutrition, health and wellness and to create a more sustainable future. Instead of it's mission was to pursuit of profits aim, it had also achieved specific sustainability commitment and progress in the categories of nutrition, environmental impact and water use, social impact, rural development and responsible sourcing to meet the needs of it's wider of groups of stakeholders' aim. On the nutrition, health and wellness aspect, Nestle met the needs to its stakeholder (clients), such as, Nestle rolled out new portion guidance tools and launched an educational campaign and balance your plate to help consumers build nutritious and delicious and convenient meals that met the dietary guidelines for Americans; Nestle also reduced sodium content in many of its most popular brands, such as Stouffer's and DiGiorno and committed to further reduce sodium content by 10 percent in products that did not meet the Nestle; Nestle also reduced sugar content, such as ninety six percent of Nestle 's children's products met the Nestle criteria for low sugar and by the end of 2014 year, 100 percent of children's products would meet these criteria as well as Nestle also removed trans-fat content, such as Nestle committed to reach zero food and beverage products with trans-fat originating to use as functional ingredients by 2016 year. It seemed that Nestle had considered its food and beverage production content whether these content would have negative influence to its stakeholder (clients) nowadays (Adrian, P. 2012).

On the environmental impact aspect, Nestle reduced waste during it's food and beverage products were producing. As part of its commitment to eliminate all forms of waste, Nestle reduced 44 percent of waste per ton of product since 2010 year in the USA five factory locations reached zero waste to landfill status by the end of 2013 year; Nestle also considered responsible packaging responsibility, such as Nestle Waters North America led the USA bottled water industry in light weighting packaging, in part by reducing the plastic content of its 1/2 liter bottles by 60 percent since 1994 year. Since 2003 year alone, more than 3.3 billion pounds of plastic had been saved by Nestle as well as Nestle also adopted responsible sourcing, such as Nestle Purina Pet Care implemented responsible sourcing guidelines for seafood that align with Nestle 's global responsible sourcing guidelines, working with experts to track suppliers and contribute to healthier ecosystem. In 2013 year, Nestle also reached an important target for palm oil, with 100 percent of palm oil now Round table on sustainable palm oil certified. It seemed that Nestle also considerate whether environment would have negative influence occurrence during it's production (Adrian, P. 2012).

On social impact aspect, Nestle supported local communities, such as Nestle in USA donated more than $2.3 million dollars to support local United Way organizations; It also provided disaster relief, such as Nestle waters donated more than 685,000 bottled of water and Nestle Purina contributed more than 60,000 pounds of pet food and 41,000 pounds of cat little to local shelters across the USA for disaster relief as well as it grew supplier diversity, such as Nestle works with over 4,100 small, minority, women and veteran owned businesses to help to spur local economies. It seemed that Nestle also considerate social needs. Thus, it is seemed Nestle company have managed to sustainable reconcile these two aims to pursuit profit as well as it also could gave positive influence to its stakeholders. Such as consumer could feel safe to enjoy to eat Nestle company's health foods; societies could be reduced unemployment from its outsourced assistance job to partners; natural environment could be reduced pollution from its productive protection. Hence, it was not actually neglect its shareholders' benefits during it was doing business as the same time (Adrian, P. 2012).

What are basic lessons in marketing that the Body Shop might have taken on board in its early years in order to improve its chances of long term success?

The body shop is a global manufacturer and retailer of naturally inspired , ethically produced beauty and cosmetics products. Founded in the UK in 1976 year by Dame Anita Roddick, who now have 2,133 stores in 55 countries with a range of over 1,200 products in Europe, America, Middle East, Asia and Africa. However, the body shop has not entered the China market. It takes a strong position on activism, ethical business, human rights and environmentalism in a global perspective. The body shop is banned in China because cosmetics sold there have to be tested on animals, according to Roddick. In, 2006 when it was bought by the French cosmetics company L'Oreal which is a big player in China. China has launched scientific developing strategy for future the current policies of advocating. Hence, it is the perfect time for the body shop to enter China market. However, prior to that, as an independent member of the L'Oreal family, the body shop has to make decisions on differentiation marketing strategies, market segmentation and marketing position (Adrian, P. 2012).

It might have taken two purposes to body shop marketing in its early years in order to improve its chances from short term to long term success. The short term objective was to generate more sales for the body shop. Through, the introduction of a new service, the market up class, it was hoped that clients could try and experience the body shop cosmetic products. Positive experience of using its products could then be developed through their trial using the market up class. It was estimated that this positive experience could push up the sales.

The long term objective was to educate the belief of the body shop to the young potential clients, so that who would become those who preferred natural cosmetic products and were loyal to the body shop in the future. Objectives could provide the starting point for marketing plans and strategies and should be specific targets that are obtained but also challenging. Specific, measurable, agreed, realistic and time related objectives might be taken to body shop to improve early years in chances in long term success. It seemed that Hong Kong was one good market for body shop to satisfy an unfulfilled customers needs to pursue body shop investment chance. Therefore, the objective were to push up sales and built a loyal customer basis for the future. For example, Hong Kong was one young student clients growth market to body shop. In the past, one cosmetic products market statistic was indicated that the colour cosmetic retail value had been increasing from 2002 year, HK$938.3 million dollars to 2007 year, HK$1,132,3 million dollars, so percentage was increased to 5.12% . (Adrian, P. 2012).

It seemed Hong Kong might be one good skin cosmetic care products developed market to this body shop in early years. The another factor might improve body shop long term success factor was whether body shop had attempted to analyze direct competition. The body shop's direct competition was not from the name brand like Dior, Chanel or Olay, but rather the less well known brands, from Japan or Korea. Along with the great impact of Korean fashion, many Korean cosmetics brands like Missha and the Face shop had already established shops in China. These two brands also promoted their natural ingredients and target the young customer segment as what the body shop products competition concept could be offered to a market to satisfy a want or need and offered five levels, which were the core benefits, basic product, expected product, augmented product and potential product. Each level added more customer value and the five constitute client value hierarchy products of these three brands were all using natural ingredients and simple and natural in packaging. The body shop , however, differentiated itself at the top levels of the five product and transformations the products might undergo in the future.

Marketing management and planning was essential to body shop, it was the implementation of strategies to achieve long run profitability to body shop and growth. When body shop was looking at how it would achieve this in early years in order to improve the chances long term success, its two keys points to consider are:

What was body shop man activity at a particular time? And how it would reach its goals? It might design a strategy that insured a consistent approach to offer its skin care products to raise competition in mind the skin care products changing market. These included product line, distribution methods, marketing communication and pricing. For example, achieving marketing research to Hong Kong and China skin care products market to analyze what were these factors to influence these country people who felt needs to buy its skin care products: Such as internal factors include personality, motivation, learning, perception and attitude; external factors included culture, social class, reference groups , family and personal influences and situational factors included time, income, mobility and availability. The reason was because due to consumers bought skin care products to protect whose skin (core benefits) and their expectations if who were willing to pay more basic product. To enhance the product level, body shop skin health product needed emphasize that skin products were natural. Products of the body shop offered the same effective and natural and flavor and unique corporate values. Body shop was mostly natural (augmented level). Far more than the visible products, the shop shop's unique corporate values create the potential value to fulfil customer's desire of making a better health world. It's good corporate desire citizenship went beyond supplying rational and emotional benefits. Body shop might enter China market to improve long term success. The body shop divided its markets to include overseas Pacific Europe, America , Australia and New Zealand, Middle East, Africa and local UK countries. Adrian, P.(2012) indicated that a sampling questionnaire survey was conducted among 200 consumers, ranging from 18 to 50 ages in May 2006, a total of 170 valid responses that were used for analysis. Among the 170 responses, 66% were females. The findings were:

(1) About 60 % hoped that cosmetics could be a symbol of being environmental friendly.

(2) 90% would choose products made of natural ingredients.

(3) 90% spent less than 300 RMB on cosmetics and skin care products quarterly.

(4) 83% Chinese youth (age range from 18 to 25 ages) were innovators and conscious of environment.

Hence, the body shop might take a share of potential market in China. It should launch its products among younger cosmetic industry were young females who chased beauty and were willing to spend money on it. So, packaging was one of the vital factors in attracting client. The body shop took a unique approach by choosing simple packaging. The package was not made for mature women. It was made for young female students, who could enjoy on international brand at an inexpensive cost. The body shop was not only to meet young people's demand for beauty , but the demand of being responsible to environment and human rights. Hence, the target market of the body shop should focus on young people ageing from 15 ages to 30 ages. Hence, body shop might take marketing research in Hong Kong and China market to have more confident to invest in these market to improve more success.

Next, Whether body shop might achieve price strategy to improve to raise success chance. An assumption is when the individual client is considering the price of any a body shop's beauty skin health product. Economic theory suggests that the customer will act in a totally rational economic manner, such that body shop's every client total utility (or satisfaction) is maximized. In deciding whether try or not try body shop's product, which totally rational consumer will carefully equate whether ought to buy or ought not buy body shop's product at the asking price set will maximizing whose utility. In making judgment, the economist assumes that the consumer has perfect information about both the prices and utility of all the other competitive products in the market and that price is the only consideration in choice. Clearly there are unrealistic assumptions. Price could be determined easily when a target market was identified. (Adrian, P. 2012)

From survey indicated 64% of the 170 responses spent less than 1000 RMB on cosmetics and skin care every quarter and 24% of their expenditure was between 100 RMB and 300 RMB on cosmetics an skin care. This number could not be ignored if a cosmetics company wanted to enter this large market and be a leader. For the younger generation, the prices of the products could not be high. The price of these main competitors ranges from 10RMB to 200 RMB. The prices in Hong Kong have higher than that in the USA or the UK. And the consumer's purchasing power in mainland China is much lower than that of Hong Kong . Hence, body shop should adopt a price range in China which was similar to that of the USA or the UK rather than of Hong Kong. Once the body shop established greatly reduced and the capability of price adjustment would be achieved accordingly.

Further, body shop might have chain stores selling channel strategy to attempt to achieve long term success. Sample survey revealed that supermarket was for Chinese to purchase skin care and cosmetics. 120 out of the 170 responses hoped that who could choose products from the chain stores in the future, which suggested that the body shop should build up its own stores was regarded as cares about corporate culture and corporate image. It insisted on selling in its own stores rather than setting up counters in a shopping mall. The stores of body shop could be found easily worldwide because of stores were importance in this competitive buyer. Hence, in China, its appearance should be same as worldwide. Some housewives joined the body shop as sales agent and hold sales parties for other housewives. The sales channel allowed the body shop to reach out to more clients by bringing the store directly into client's homes. This would be a totally new method of marketing in China, but it offered a good opportunity for women to choose products and share feedback in a relaxed atmosphere. This fresh concept could attract female consumers. Nowadays, students in China could only obtain famous skin care products and cosmetics brands from campus agents, as who could not afford the products sold over the counters. It was a major problem that agents could not guarantee the ingredients and the quality of the goods. If the body shop could hold small parties to share products and opinions, that would be a good way to boost sales among students. Hence, body shop might take price strategy to Hong Kong and china market to predict whether what price who could accept to raise more confident to invest to this market to improve more success.

Further, body shop might also have promotion strategy to attempt to achieve long term success. The body shop adopted environmental friendly manufacturing, opposed abuses of human rights and was accountable for its actions. The unique values attracted numbers of media groups in many countries. This results in its establishing a good reputation without any advertisements. The body shop also joined numerous social causes, which substitute advertisements. In China, however, it was totally different. In this brand new market, most people were out aware of this company. If it carried on a marketing promotion of no commercials it was impossible to reach a high market share. Hence, commercial advertisements were needed in China. The body shop could use this advertisement to give on impression that women should care about their well being both mentally and physically and it had created a sexy grand with simple packaging and without objectifying women. Many brands reach customers directly by colorful commercials and show their products in movies and TV play series. For the sakes of brand image, some movies about human rights , environmental protection and animal protection could be chosen by the body shop as carriers for particular commercial as most of the audiences were well educated, well paid and environmentally concerned.

The target consumers of the body shop aged from 20 to 40 ages were energetic , knowledgeable and environmentally concerned. The body shop could give some lectures on makeup or skin care on campuses to raise feeling among students. To reach brand awareness and high brand loyalty , some samples should be given to students by experience marketing approach. Hence, body shop might take promotion to Hong Kong and China schools to let many young people to know why who needed to buy skin care products to protect their body skin to persuade who felt more needs. In conclusion, the body shop was famous for creating a niche market sector for naturally inspired skin care and cosmetic products through it's unique corporate values worldwide. The significance of the body shop's early entry into China market were strongly proposed. Once the body shop decided to enter the China market, the relevant marketing strategies and management should be implemented, such as the market segmentation and market positioning with the proper consideration of Chinese consumers should be studied in order to win the mind share of potential Chinese customers with the right marketing strategies. Overall, the findings of market survey and theoretical analysis strategy support the feasibility of the body shop's early entry into China market.

CHAPTER TEN

Reasons of societal marketing orientation may help body shop to raise sale price

What is the difference between production orientation and societal marketing orientation and sales orientation to body shop ?

Critically assess the extent to which whether Body Shop to be a truly marketing oriented organization throughout its 30 years history.The body shop international power line carrier (the body shop) was founded by Dame Anita Roddick in the England in 1976. It sold personal beauty care products, such as baby and child specific products, bath and shower and colour cosmetics, deodorants, skin care, hair care, fragrances, sun care etc skin health products to provide human body benefits. Nowadays, the body shop was skin and body care manufacturer and retailer operating in 55 countries with over 2,100 stores. It had 42 exclusive outlets in Hong Kong. It's missions were to dedicate to pursuit of social and environment change to meaningfully contribute to local, national and international communities in which trade to passionately campaign for the protection of the environment, human and civil rights and against animal testing and to make fun, passion and care part of our daily lives (Adrian, P. 2012).

There are five main marketing orientations of which a company will adopt one. This will determine the way it interacts with the customer. Such as product orientation suggests that a company focuses inwards looking at what it is capable of, rather than the needs and wants of the client; sales orientation is based upon selling existing products with a turnover sale numbers relationship marketing orientation recognizes the value of repeat business over, not only with customers but suppliers as well; societal marketing orientation is relatively new in the scheme of things but suggests on top of meeting the needs and wants of the customer and the organization there is the societies interests to be looked and marketing orientation is based around the needs and wants of a customer to meet business objectives and it assumes that a sale depends on a customer's decision to purchase a product or provide a service.

● What is marketing two levels meaning ?

Marketing can be seen at two levels, the first level is such as a business philosophy, marketing puts customers at the center of an organization's consideration and which is reflected in basic values , such as the requirement to understand and respond to customers' needs and the necessary to search constantly for new market opportunity. In a truly marketing oriented organization, these values are instilled in all employees and should influence their behavior without any need for prompting. The personnel manager would have a selection policy that recruited staff who could fulfil the needs of customers rather than simply minimizing the wage bill in any marketing oriented organization. The other level is techniques of marketing also include pricing, the design of channels of distribution and new product development.

● What are the three components of market orientation ?

The assessing the nature and importance of market orientation for large firms, such as body shop. The three components of market orientation could be analytically separated. The components of market orientation organization include the first component is the customer orientation, it means an organization must have a thorough understanding of its target buyers, so that it can create a product of superior value to give client benefits ; the second component is the competitor orientation, it means any firm should look at how well its competitors are able to satisfy buyers' needs. It should understand the short term strengths and weaknesses and long term capabilities and strategies of current and potential competitors as well as the third component is to develop marketing plans that are not acted upon by people who are capable of delivering promises made to customers and a marketing orientation organization requires that the organization draws upon and integrates its human and physical resources effectively and adapts them to meet client's needs. Otherwise, a production and sales orientation may be appropriate to firms at certain stages in the evolution of markets. Where the dominant business environment is based on the need for good production planning above all, the company that does this best will achieve the greatest overall business success.

It is either production orientation, it means organizations that produce what they imagined consumers wanted, rather than what they actually wanted. Planning for full utilization of capital equipment are often seen as more important than ensuring that equipment is used to provide goods and services that people actually wants. Production-oriented firms generally aim for efficiency in production rather than effectiveness in meeting customer's needs . It is either or selling orientation, it means advertising, sales promotion and personal selling techniques are used to emphasize product differentiation and brands and it does not focus on satisfying client needs or desire new product offerings and production led. Hence, one market orientation organization needs to focus on satisfying clients‘ needs profitably by these marketing mix, such as product, price, place, physical evidence, processed, people and promotion. Anyway ,Market orientation implied that body shop , which ought seek information about clients, such as current and future needs and took action based this information (client orientation); it ought seek information about competitors' current strengths and weaknesses and their long term strategies and took actions based on these information (competitor orientation) ; it ought coordinate the actions taken by sharing clients and competitors information internally (intra-firm communication).

● What is the three components of market orientation ?

The three components of market orientation meant social marketing and understanding boarder concerns and ethical environmental, legal and social context of marketing activities and programs. The cause and effects of marketing clearly beyond the company and the consumer to society as whole. New terms humanistic marketing and ecological marketing were suggested to societal marketing concept.

● What is the social marketing concept ?

The social marketing concept holds that the organization's task is to determine the needs, wants and interests of target markets and to deliver the desired satisfactions more effectively and
efficiently than competitors and the society's welling being, such as body shop had achieved sales and profit gains by adopting and practicing a form of the societal marketing concept called cause related marketing.

● DISCUSSION

Body Shop is marketing orientation organization in 30 years.Critically assess the extent to which I consider Body Shop to be a truly marketing oriented organization throughout its 30 years history . It seemed body shop had achieved cause-related marketing as an opportunity to enhance their corporate reputation, raised brand awareness, increased customer loyalty and built sales. It's corporate values were composed of five core values. The first one was to oppose animal testing. The opposing animal testing for both cosmetic products and ingredients began in 1976 years.

In the 1980 year and 1990 year, who successfully campaigned with animal protection groups to change the UK and European laws to support the development products were tried on human volunteers. Along with the development of technology testing had played a leading role to protect the rights of both human and animals . The second one was to support community trade, it initiated the trade not aid objective of creating trade to help people in the third world utilizing their resources to their own needs. This reflects communities needed a fair price for natural ingredients who purchased from these often marginalized countries. The third one was to activate self esteem. Women were the main customers and employees in the body shop. The fourth one was to defend human rights. The body shop had long campaign on human rights, highlighting abuses and increasing the global awareness of issues by making full use of the geographic advantages of their shops and supporting other human rights organizations. The last one was protect our plant. In 2001 year, huge campaign against global warming was hosted by the body shop and green peace, who advocated the use of recyclable source and materials (Adrian, P. 2012). Although profits were an essential element of long run survival in body shop and it was likely to be overall corporate and marketing objectives, but body shop seemed more to be required level of profits rather than profit that there were many other objectives, which might pursue through its pricing strategies . For example, if body shop wanted to maximize market share or simply survive, a different set of prices would be delivered than if the objectives were to maximize profits. Hence, body shop ought to see viewpoint the marketing side of pricing and it ought not to see viewpoint the production / supply side of pricing if it was a truly marketing oriented organization.

The key inputs for body shop to make pricing decision whether it was marketing oriented or productive / supply oriented included production objectives or marketing objectives, demand or supply numbers were considered cost or sale price and competitors or clients consideration factors, such as beauty skin care products in competitive markets demand, i.e. To decide the price whether customers are willing and able to pay is a major consideration in the selection of pricing strategies and levels of demands . Hence, body shop ought to consider demand numbers , it ought not consider production / supply numbers if it was a truly marketing oriented organization. For example, since most of the body shop's factories were still located in the UK, where wages and salaries were much higher than in Asia, so UK itself sale product prices were higher than that from Asia itself sale product prices.

I think Body Shop was a truly marketing oriented organization more than production/supply oriented organization throughout its 30 years history. In fact, Body Shop was experiencing market level growth. It could expand its sales market in Europe, America, Middle East, Asia and Africa etc different countries. It seemed that it had attempted to carry on marketing research to decide to choose which countries would have more client numbers to demand to buy its personal care products, then it would follow the countries' estimated client numbers to produce its products to sell to the countries. So, it was why some Asia countries sold its bath and shower and skin and hair care and colour cosmetics products more than its fragrances products, such as Hong Kong young people were more acceptable to use bath and show and color cosmetic and skin and hair care products more than fragrances products . It seemed that Hong Kong Body Shop sold fragrance products numbers were less than bath and shower and color cosmetics etc. products. Nowadays, I think the personal beauty care products new businesses which planned to entry this market was more difficult. It was possible than Body Shop was a famous personal beauty care products sale company, it had owned many clients too many years. So , it caused barriers to any new personal beauty care product competitors felt difficult to entry this market .Furthermore, Body Shop had build strong buyer and seller power to increase clients had more confident to use its products, it was possible that who felt its different kind of products could give more health to their skin or body more than other similar personal beauty care products. Moreover, I believe Body Shop had attempted to carry on technological experimenting to aim to build different countries' clients had more confident to use its products forever.

In conclusion, it seemed that Body Shop was truly marketing oriented organization more than productive/ supply oriented organization oriented organization throughout its 30 years history.

Any companies need to consider the social responsibility during which are the pursuits of profit and meeting the needs of wider group of stakeholders incompatible. Without this self interest, there will be little motivation for firms to provide better services, workers couldn't earn better salaries and clients couldn't aspire for a high level of consumption. Hence, self interest which helps markets work more effectively for the benefits of all. Hence, companies should adopt a code of behavior and conduct and ethical behavior which would not influence any stakeholders groups' benefits to pursuit their profit honestly. Corporate social responsibility is a form of corporate self regulation integrated into a business model. It aims to give responsibility for corporate actions and to encourage a positive impact on the environment and stakeholders including consumers, employees, investors, communities and others and it is titled to aid an organization's mission as well as guide to what the company can give the best benefits to serve its customers. I shall use body shop company as one example to judge whether what extent are the pursuits of profit and meeting the needs of wider groups of stakeholders will be incompatible.

In fact, body shop could adopt a code of behavior and conduct and ethical behavior which would not influence any stakeholders groups' benefits to pursuit their profit honestly. Such as, one of the major and most successful initiatives which body shop used an effective supply chain for their products and body shop made use of their sustainable chain supply strategy to ensure that there was the promotion and the maintenance of the social ethical behavior in its business. Hence, it seemed that body shop could be compatible to achieve an effective supply chain to deliver to different countries' stores to meet clients who had more need to buy different kinds of skin care products to provide them to choose to buy in the reasonable price choices in the short time. It is therefore in the best practices and interests for body shop to reach out to the communities in their businesses to provide raw materials to help the manufacturers of the beauty products. It also partook in the development of the market for such small scale suppliers. In many cases the body shop tried to outsource its raw materials to its customers. This had ensured the sustainability of its customer base this included it's sensitivity to its environment and the required standards of the labor practices of its partners. Hence, it seemed that body shop could be compatible to help its partners to earn profits and any countries' partners could provide more job chances to unemployed people to work from body shop's outsourcing strategy.

Hence, this had been developed by the body shop by including strategies, such as third party logistic providers and intermediaries in which who had no ownership. The body shop was a multinational company also adopted trading to purchasing approach where it shifted from short term where focus of buying articles to long term focus of fewer suppliers. This was an attempt of it to develop quality products where prices were also fair and affordable to sell to different countries‘ clients. It seemed that body shop could be compatible to sell reasonable prices of products to it's clients. Moreover, it had included in its strategies the aspect of business promotion using catalogues. For the same reason, it had been involved in printing of catalogues which were given out to the clients with their purchases. It was important to note that it' catalogues always contained all it's information descriptions and any person who purchased it's products was bound to receive the explanation of all it's product. This was an attempt of it to develop quality products where prices were also fair and affordable to sell to different countries‘ clients. It seemed that body shop could be compatible to provide clear information description in catalogues to let whose clients to know what it's different kinds of style body skin care products ingredients and benefits were , then who could compare it's products to other competitors to decide to buy or not buy fairly.

In Oct. 2007 the campaign for safe cosmetic products, in which 25 multinational companies participated, tested 33 brand name lipsticks and found one-third of the sampled exceeded the limit of lead allowed in confectionery. The affected brands included L'Oreal and Christian Dior. A definite effect would be that consumers would be more concerned regarded the ingredients of products who used, which was likely to have an effect on cosmetics and skin care products were released to capture share. It seemed body shop needed to consider its beauty personal care products were the most ensure to own organic ingredients to let any countries clients (stakeholder) to meet their body health care needs (Adrian, P. 2012).

On the health and natural aspect, body shop had health and safe responsibility to consumers. Although, I felt who had considered this issue because it had 30 years history to operate this business and it had not received any serious negative complaints damage its health product image from clients before. However, with consumers were increasingly informed and were educated, who were now more demanding for more information regarding products and were becoming more aware of health issue.

Products with organic ingredients and natural ingredients, such as tea and plants were gaining popular. Furthermore, consumers were looking for healthier substitutes to seemingly unhealthy products, such as color cosmetics. Hence, body shop began to sell the reducing numbers, it was possible due to clients compared it's body care products quality to the other competitors and who felt it's product's ingredients existed some poor ingredients to cause every one's body to be unhealthy.

Hence, it's productive processing was very important. It seemed that body shop could be compatible to consider its individual client body skin health issue whether after who had used it's body skin care products to have skin hurt or skin pain feeling. In conclusion, to judge what extent are the pursuits of profit and meeting the needs of wider groups of stakeholders incompatible for any individual business, it is depended on whether the company's any stakeholders, such as employees, clients, suppliers, partners, society (communities) etc. who will have positive or negative influence from it. I feel that it will be incompatible if the company give negative influence to any one of its stakeholder. Hence, if any one company's at least one stakeholder who felt who had negative influence due to it did business to relate to whom unwillingly, then it's pursuit of profits aim would be incompatible to meet it's needs of its any one of stakeholder. Such as body shop will give positive influence to its all stakeholders. Hence, I feel it is compatible extent to pursuit of profit and meeting the needs of its wider groups of stakeholders definitely.

I feel that Nestle company has managed to sustainable reconcile to pursuit profits and meeting the needs of its wider groups of stakeholders two aims compatibly. Nestle was the world's largest food and beverage company. Nestle in the United States, which represented seven operating across the USA country and it was the first expanded effort in USA and achievement tied to Nestle 's global sustainability principle and commitment. Nowadays, It served 97% of American householders and Nestle 's mission was to lead the industry in nutrition, health and wellness and to create a more sustainable future. Instead of it's mission was to pursuit of profits aim, it had also achieved specific sustainability commitment and progress in the categories of nutrition, environmental impact and water use, social impact, rural development and responsible sourcing to meet the needs of it's wider of groups of stakeholders' aim. On the nutrition, health and wellness aspect, Nestle met the needs to its stakeholder (clients), such as, Nestle rolled out new portion guidance tools and launched an educational campaign and balance your plate to help consumers build nutritious and delicious and convenient meals that met the dietary guidelines for Americans; Nestle also reduced sodium content in many of its most popular brands, such as Stouffer's and DiGiorno and committed to further reduce sodium content by 10 percent in products that did not meet the Nestle; Nestle also reduced sugar content, such as ninety six percent of Nestle 's children's products met the Nestle criteria for low sugar and by the end of 2014 year, 100 percent of children's products would meet these criteria as well as Nestle also removed trans-fat content, such as Nestle committed to reach zero food and beverage products with trans-fat originating to use as functional ingredients by 2016 year. It seemed that Nestle had considered its food and beverage production content whether these content would have negative influence to its stakeholder (clients) nowadays (Adrian, P. 2012).

On the environmental impact aspect, Nestle reduced waste during it's food and beverage products were producing. As part of its commitment to eliminate all forms of waste, Nestle reduced 44 percent of waste per ton of product since 2010 year in the USA five factory locations reached zero waste to landfill status by the end of 2013 year; Nestle also considered responsible packaging responsibility, such as Nestle Waters North America led the USA bottled water industry in light weighting packaging, in part by reducing the plastic content of its 1/2 liter bottles by 60 percent since 1994 year. Since 2003 year alone, more than 3.3 billion pounds of plastic had been saved by Nestle as well as Nestle also adopted responsible sourcing, such as Nestle Purina Pet Care implemented responsible sourcing guidelines for seafood that align with Nestle 's global responsible sourcing guidelines, working with experts to track suppliers and contribute to healthier ecosystem. In 2013 year, Nestle also reached an important target for palm oil, with 100 percent of palm oil now Round table on sustainable palm oil certified. It seemed that Nestle also considerate whether environment would have negative influence occurrence during it's production (Adrian, P. 2012).

On social impact aspect, Nestle supported local communities, such as Nestle in USA donated more than $2.3 million dollars to support local United Way organizations; It also provided disaster relief, such as Nestle waters donated more than 685,000 bottled of water and Nestle Purina contributed more than 60,000 pounds of pet food and 41,000 pounds of cat little to local shelters across the USA for disaster relief as well as it grew supplier diversity, such as Nestle works with over 4,100 small, minority, women and veteran owned businesses to help to spur local economies. It seemed that Nestle also considerate social needs. Thus, it is seemed Nestle company have managed to sustainable reconcile these two aims to pursuit profit as well as it also could gave positive influence to its stakeholders. Such as consumer could feel safe to enjoy to eat Nestle company's health foods; societies could be reduced unemployment from its outsourced assistance job to partners; natural environment could be reduced pollution from its productive protection. Hence, it was not actually neglect its shareholders' benefits during it was doing business as the same time (Adrian, P. 2012).

What are basic lessons in marketing that the Body Shop might have taken on board in its early years in order to improve its chances of long term success?

The body shop is a global manufacturer and retailer of naturally inspired , ethically produced beauty and cosmetics products. Founded in the UK in 1976 year by Dame Anita Roddick, who now have 2,133 stores in 55 countries with a range of over 1,200 products in Europe, America, Middle East, Asia and Africa. However, the body shop has not entered the China market. It takes a strong position on activism, ethical business, human rights and environmentalism in a global perspective. The body shop is banned in China because cosmetics sold there have to be tested on animals, according to Roddick. In, 2006 when it was bought by the French cosmetics company L'Oreal which is a big player in China. China has launched scientific developing strategy for future the current policies of advocating. Hence, it is the perfect time for the body shop to enter China market. However, prior to that, as an independent member of the L'Oreal family, the body shop has to make decisions on differentiation marketing strategies, market segmentation and marketing position (Adrian, P. 2012).

It might have taken two purposes to body shop marketing in its early years in order to improve its chances from short term to long term success. The short term objective was to generate more sales for the body shop. Through, the introduction of a new service, the market up class, it was hoped that clients could try and experience the body shop cosmetic products. Positive experience of using its products could then be developed through their trial using the market up class. It was estimated that this positive experience could push up the sales.

The long term objective was to educate the belief of the body shop to the young potential clients, so that who would become those who preferred natural cosmetic products and were loyal to the body shop in the future. Objectives could provide the starting point for marketing plans and strategies and should be specific targets that are obtained but also challenging. Specific, measurable, agreed, realistic and time related objectives might be taken to body shop to improve early years in chances in long term success. It seemed that Hong Kong was one good market for body shop to satisfy an unfulfilled customers needs to pursue body shop investment chance. Therefore, the objective were to push up sales and built a loyal customer basis for the future. For example, Hong Kong was one young student clients growth market to body shop. In the past, one cosmetic products market statistic was indicated that the colour cosmetic retail value had been increasing from 2002 year, HK$938.3 million dollars to 2007 year, HK$1,132,3 million dollars, so percentage was increased to 5.12% . (Adrian, P. 2012).

It seemed Hong Kong might be one good skin cosmetic care products developed market to this body shop in early years. The another factor might improve body shop long term success factor was whether body shop had attempted to analyze direct competition. The body shop's direct competition was not from the name brand like Dior, Chanel or Olay, but rather the less well known brands, from Japan or Korea. Along with the great impact of Korean fashion, many Korean cosmetics brands like Missha and the Face shop had already established shops in China. These two brands also promoted their natural ingredients and target the young customer segment as what the body shop products competition concept could be offered to a market to satisfy a want or need and offered five levels, which were the core benefits, basic product, expected product, augmented product and potential product. Each level added more customer value and the five constitute client value hierarchy products of these three brands were all using natural ingredients and simple and natural in packaging. The body shop , however, differentiated itself at the top levels of the five product and transformations the products might undergo in the future.

Marketing management and planning was essential to body shop, it was the implementation of strategies to achieve long run profitability to body shop and growth. When body shop was looking at how it would achieve this in early years in order to improve the chances long term success, its two keys points to consider are:

What was body shop man activity at a particular time? And how it would reach its goals? It might design a strategy that insured a consistent approach to offer its skin care products to raise competition in mind the skin care products changing market. These included product line, distribution methods, marketing communication and pricing. For example, achieving marketing research to Hong Kong and China skin care products market to analyze what were these factors to influence these country people who felt needs to buy its skin care products: Such as internal factors include personality, motivation, learning, perception and attitude; external factors included culture, social class, reference groups , family and personal influences and situational factors included time, income, mobility and availability. The reason was because due to consumers bought skin care products to protect whose skin (core benefits) and their expectations if who were willing to pay more basic product. To enhance the product level, body shop skin health product needed emphasize that skin products were natural. Products of the body shop offered the same effective and natural and flavor and unique corporate values. Body shop was mostly natural (augmented level). Far more than the visible products, the shop shop's unique corporate values create the potential value to fulfil customer's desire of making a better health world. It's good corporate desire citizenship went beyond supplying rational and emotional benefits. Body shop might enter China market to improve long term success. The body shop divided its markets to include overseas Pacific Europe, America , Australia and New Zealand, Middle East, Africa and local UK countries. Adrian, P.(2012) indicated that a sampling questionnaire survey was conducted among 200 consumers, ranging from 18 to 50 ages in May 2006, a total of 170 valid responses that were used for analysis. Among the 170 responses, 66% were females. The findings were:

(1) About 60 % hoped that cosmetics could be a symbol of being environmental friendly.

(2) 90% would choose products made of natural ingredients.

(3) 90% spent less than 300 RMB on cosmetics and skin care products quarterly.

(4) 83% Chinese youth (age range from 18 to 25 ages) were innovators and conscious of environment.

Hence, the body shop might take a share of potential market in China. It should launch its products among younger cosmetic industry were young females who chased beauty and were willing to spend money on it. So, packaging was one of the vital factors in attracting client. The body shop took a unique approach by choosing simple packaging. The package was not made for mature women. It was made for young female students, who could enjoy on international brand at an inexpensive cost. The body shop was not only to meet young people's demand for beauty , but the demand of being responsible to environment and human rights. Hence, the target market of the body shop should focus on young people ageing from 15 ages to 30 ages. Hence, body shop might take marketing research in Hong Kong and China market to have more confident to invest in these market to improve more success.

Next, Whether body shop might achieve price strategy to improve to raise success chance. An assumption is when the individual client is considering the price of any a body shop's beauty skin health product. Economic theory suggests that the customer will act in a totally rational economic manner, such that body shop's every client total utility (or satisfaction) is maximized. In deciding whether try or not try body shop's product, which totally rational consumer will carefully equate whether ought to buy or ought not buy body shop's product at the asking price set will maximizing whose utility. In making judgment, the economist assumes that the consumer has perfect information about both the prices and utility of all the other competitive products in the market and that price is the only consideration in choice. Clearly there are unrealistic assumptions. Price could be determined easily when a target market was identified. (Adrian, P. 2012)

From survey indicated 64% of the 170 responses spent less than 1000 RMB on cosmetics and skin care every quarter and 24% of their expenditure was between 100 RMB and 300 RMB on cosmetics an skin care. This number could not be ignored if a cosmetics company wanted to enter this large market and be a leader. For the younger generation, the prices of the products could not be high. The price of these main competitors ranges from 10RMB to 200 RMB. The prices in Hong Kong have higher than that in the USA or the UK. And the consumer's purchasing power in mainland China is much lower than that of Hong Kong . Hence, body shop should adopt a price range in China which was similar to that of the USA or the UK rather than of Hong Kong. Once the body shop established greatly reduced and the capability of price adjustment would be achieved accordingly.

Further, body shop might have chain stores selling channel strategy to attempt to achieve long term success. Sample survey revealed that supermarket was for Chinese to purchase skin care and cosmetics. 120 out of the 170 responses hoped that who could choose products from the chain stores in the future, which suggested that the body shop should build up its own stores was regarded as cares about corporate culture and corporate image. It insisted on selling in its own stores rather than setting up counters in a shopping mall. The stores of body shop could be found easily worldwide because of stores were importance in this competitive buyer. Hence, in China, its appearance should be same as worldwide. Some housewives joined the body shop as sales agent and hold sales parties for other housewives. The sales channel allowed the body shop to reach out to more clients by bringing the store directly into client's homes. This would be a totally new method of marketing in China, but it offered a good opportunity for women to choose products and share feedback in a relaxed atmosphere. This fresh concept could attract female consumers. Nowadays, students in China could only obtain famous skin care products and cosmetics brands from campus agents, as who could not afford the products sold over the counters. It was a major problem that agents could not guarantee the ingredients and the quality of the goods. If the body shop could hold small parties to share products and opinions, that would be a good way to boost sales among students. Hence, body shop might take price strategy to Hong Kong and china market to predict whether what price who could accept to raise more confident to invest to this market to improve more success.

Further, body shop might also have promotion strategy to attempt to achieve long term success. The body shop adopted environmental friendly manufacturing, opposed abuses of human rights and was accountable for its actions. The unique values attracted numbers of media groups in many countries. This results in its establishing a good reputation without any advertisements. The body shop also joined numerous social causes, which substitute advertisements. In China, however, it was totally different. In this brand new market, most people were out aware of this company. If it carried on a marketing promotion of no commercials it was impossible to reach a high market share. Hence, commercial advertisements were needed in China. The body shop could use this advertisement to give on impression that women should care about their well being both mentally and physically and it had created a sexy grand with simple packaging and without objectifying women. Many brands reach customers directly by colorful commercials and show their products in movies and TV play series. For the sakes of brand image, some movies about human rights , environmental protection and animal protection could be chosen by the body shop as carriers for particular commercial as most of the audiences were well educated, well paid and environmentally concerned.

The target consumers of the body shop aged from 20 to 40 ages were energetic , knowledgeable and environmentally concerned. The body shop could give some lectures on makeup or skin care on campuses to raise feeling among students. To reach brand awareness and high brand loyalty , some samples should be given to students by experience marketing approach. Hence, body shop might take promotion to Hong Kong and China schools to let many young people to know why who needed to buy skin care products to protect their body skin to persuade who felt more needs. In conclusion, the body shop was famous for creating a niche market sector for naturally inspired skin care and cosmetic products through it's unique corporate values worldwide. The significance of the body shop's early entry into China market were strongly proposed. Once the body shop decided to enter the China market, the relevant marketing strategies and management should be implemented, such as the market segmentation and market positioning with the proper consideration of Chinese consumers should be studied in order to win the mind share of potential Chinese customers with the right marketing strategies. Overall, the findings of market survey and theoretical analysis strategy support the feasibility of the body shop's early entry into China market.

CHAPTER ELEVEN

Reason of sales of ready meals in supermarket may help cooking food raise sale price

Case study change in the marketing environment on sales of ready meals to supermarket, such as Walt Mark strategy ?

Using an appropriate framework of analysis, briefly summarize the effects of change in the marketing environment on sales of ready meals. Although, previously dismissed and a poor substitute for real cooking and ready meal sales have grown rapidly in recent years in many western developed countries, such as UK, France or Germany. But, Ready meal manufacturers ready to respond to a changing marketing environment. Due to one big change in recent year has been growing demand for ready prepared meals bought from a supermarket. An analysis of the reasons for the growth in the ready prepared meals markets indicates the effects of boards factors in the marketing environment on the size of a particular market. In fact, this food market is changing to drive the growth in the ready meals market, but there are differences in the food market potential between countries. The effect of change in the marketing environment on sales of ready meals, such as technology has played a big role in the growing take up of ready meals and new technologies have allowed companies to develop ready meals which preserve taste and texture, which still making them easy to use by the consumer.

Furthermore, great advances in distribution management, in particular the use of information technology to control inventories, has allowed fresh, chilled ready meals to be effectively and efficiently distributed without the need for freezing or added preservatives. Ready meals particularly appeal to single householders, which individual family members tend to eat at different times, so family meals together remains stronger in many continental European countries than in the UK individual ready meals. Young people have lost the ability to cook creatively, as cookery has been reduced in importance in the school, so young clients group will rise to buy ready meals from supermarket. Marketing can be seen as a system that must respond to environmental change. A food market can be defined as a meeting place for stakeholder (consumers) and sellers. Food market can be set up in a supermarket or restaurants. A food market consists of the individual's target taste, such as older group, family group, young group or business clients who are actual or potential caters of a restaurant meals or supermarket package of foods. Grocery stores (supermarkets) have an influence of meals (fast cooked food) outlets in low income urban areas, which has contributed to the income in access to healthy foods. An organization's marketing environment means the individuals, organizations, and forces external to the marketing management's ability to develop and maintain successful exchanges with its customers. The marketing environment to ready meal manufacturers had three levels.

Firstly, it includes the micro environment, it describes those elements that impinge directly on the ready meal manufacturers themselves, so the micro environment of ready meal manufacturers which include business clients who have direct contact, such as restaurants, supermarkets and individual clients who have direct contact. Otherwise, supermarket shoppers, restaurant clients and food supply competitors who have no direct contract to ready meal manufacturers, so who won't include in food market micro environment to ready meal manufacturers. Secondly, it includes the macro environment, it describes things that are beyond the immediate environment but can nevertheless affect an organization, so the macro environment of ready meal manufacturers which include the export countries' economies forces, such as unemployment ratio, GDP; technological forces, such as the export countries' factories food productive technology; social/ cultural forces, such as the export countries' people taste acceptance; political/legal forces, such as the export countries' import food quota numbers. Thirdly, it includes the internal environment, it describes ready meal manufacturers' employees and equipment and finance and functional responsibilities.

Environment means everything outside influences the person, in contrast with individual or personal variables . The effects of change in the marketing environment on sales of ready meals can be analyzed by creating healthy food and eating environment changing factor and supermarket technological changing factor as below:

The ready meal manufacturers could not ignore threats to the natural ecological environment change Due to the food companies could have technology to manufacture good taste cooked ready meals to provide to supermarkets to sell. Thus, it might influence the consumers to decide whether restaurants or supermarkets or ready meals suppliers who could provide the most reasonable price and taste to satisfy whose eating needs every day. Thus, it caused the growing demand for ready prepared cooked meals bought from supermarkets. Due to it was possible that consumers felt to eat ready cooked meals in expensive restaurants or who did not like to buy foods to cook from food suppliers or who could not feel which could supply more good food taste and health food quality to compare supermarkets specially. Otherwise, although, supermarkets could provide cheaper ready cooked meals to satisfy who to feel good food taste and health food quality. Due to ready meal manufacturers had new techniques to develop ready meals which preserve taste and texture, which still making them easy to use to eat by the consumers.

Furthermore, great advances in distribution management, in particular the use of information technology to control inventories, has allowed fresh , chilled ready meals to be effectively and efficiently distributed to supermarkets or restaurants without the need for freezing or added preservatives. Creating healthy food and eating environments view describes an ecological framework for conceptualizing the many food environments and conditions that influence food choices, with an emphasis on current knowledge was been regarding the home, child care, school, work site, retail store and restaurant settings. The status of measurement and evaluation of nutrition environment and the need of action to improve health are highlighted in marketing environment. More processed and convenience foods are available in large portion sizes and which were supplied at relatively low prices at supermarkets. Parents are working larger hours, there are fewer family meals and more meals are eaten away from home. The school food environment is remarkably different. It seemed that it would be changed in the marketing environment on sales of ready cooked meals to supermarket more easily. Due to supermarkets' cooked meals should focus on selling high calorie and low nutrition foods are available in multiple venues throughout the school student client group target because it was possible that supermarkets could sell ready cooked ready meals prices were more cheaper to compare to restaurants or school canters' cooked meals provided prices.

The effects of change in the marketing environment on sales of ready meals which indicated that consumers chose prefer to buy ready cooked meals from supermarkets. It seemed that a restaurant market failure could be caused to arise. For example, there was poor information on the part of food (ready cooked meals) to provide to the restaurant about the foods that consumers in a location(place) would demand for a given price to compare to the supermarket sale prices. The restaurant would lose clients if which cooked the kind of meals to sell higher price to compare to the supermarket sale of the kind of cooked ready meals price possibly. Large size supermarkets could sell cheaper ready cooked meals to low income group clients. It could cause competition to constitute a market failure to small size supermarkets. If the small size supermarkets lacked good information on the true food (ready cooked meals) with concentrations to sell cheaper prices, then this ready cooked meal market failure was one potential reason why small size supermarkets did not locate to close to the large supermarkets. Due to supermarkets grew in size would influence clients' choice to buy the numbers of cooked foods (ready meals) products. Moreover, The advent of computerized logistics and inventory systems were integrated with the large size supermarkets themselves occurred between the 1980 years and 1990 years .

So large size supermarkets were reliance on their own distribution and cooked food (ready meals) inventory systems along with larger supermarket sizes to allow super center to change to sell ready cooked meals at lower prices. Supermarkets marketing can promote healthful eating by increasing availability, affordability or restricting / de-marketing unhealthy foods to sell cooked Food (ready meals) marketing strategy at supermarkets, including labelling, packaging, pricing and point of sale advertising. Consumers' cost saving efforts and income and ready cooked meals prices increasing or decreasing factors can drive the choice of supermarkets as well as cooked meal products use of coupons and loyalty cards bargain shopping is another factor to influence their choice. Private label or store (supermarket) brands are taking an increasing share of consumers shopping dollars as the importance of brands. Supermarket shoppers stated priorities are cooked food (ready meals) quality or taste and price and healthy cooked food (ready meals) choices.

However, supermarket shoppers' buying behaviors don't always reflect on favor healthful foods. Due to demand for locally grown cooked food is increasing. Anyway, restaurant meals are changed to supermarket to sell, which decide what kinds of meals to stock and how many of different kinds of meals to stock and how much variety of kinds of meals to offer to any one supermarket as well as supermarket shoppers prefer fewer options, provided that their preferred brand or cooked food (ready meals) products are available. The designs of supermarket ready cooked meal products and packaging to supermarket to sell is the focus of unusual colors or shape which can be used to increase interest and is specially pervasive among fun foods to compare to restaurant meals. Package design, including where text and images are placed, which can influences cooked foods (supermarket ready meals repurchasing again).The influence of design differs by the type of display consumer segments seek (convenience, information or images) and ready cooked meals package sizes have a relatively strong influence on consumption; larger ready cooked meals packages might increase per-use consumption ,but smaller packages might not improve self regulation and might not actually increase total consumption.

In conclusion, I suggest that this ready meal manufacturers need to give more attention to be paid to food sellers, such as supermarkets‘ competitive differentiation and understanding the way in which customers attribute value to its ready meal products choice. Moreover, many consumers have become increasingly concerned about the health implication of the food they eat, so ready meal manufacturers will need to continue responding to such concerns. For example, who have responded with a range of low calorie meals, and addressed specific, sometimes transient, health fads, with respect to trans-fatty acids and omega 3 supplements of these cooked meal ingredients. Many consumers have also become concerned about the ecological environment and some supermarket suppliers, such as Marks and Spencer have incorporated sustainability agendas into their ready meals, for example by reducing packaging and sourcing supplies from sustainable sources. Thus, it caused ready meal manufacturers why who needed to give more attention to concern how supermarkets helped them to sell cooked ready meals in this foods market.

Critically discuss the link between the economic environment and sales of ready meals in supermarket. The macro environment, it describes things that are beyond the immediate environment but can nevertheless affect the organization. Such as the ready meal manufacturers in its macro environment, including the economic environment which can cause the manufacturers sell ready meal numbers whether which can sell more or less to different exported countries due to the exported countries' unemployment ratios, GDP and Government policies etc factors influence. Economic theory can help to explain why it can influence consumer behavior. In food sale market, it can include consumer behavior and demand side as well as retailer behavior and supply side two issues.

Consumer behavior and demand side issue, such as the exported countries' consumer whose knowledge of the nutritional benefits of foods whether which prices were raised to choose to buy reasonably as well as retailer behavior and supply side issues, such as investing for developing a restaurant or supermarket in an underserved area whether the types of meals choices which are valued or which are not valued to buy to offer to clients from imports. On the other hand, economic environment factor, individual income can influence who chooses the type, quantity and quality of food that is purchased for a house holder and it also influenced the cooking and storage facilities available in a household to influence food choice.

On the other way, economic environment variation factor can also influence food access across areas. It is important to understand the economic conditions that may contribute to food deserts, that is the costs that food retail businesses face and the choice available to consumers who want to buy foods. Economic environment factor considers the consumer and demand factors, business and supply factors and the market conditions that interact to create differences in the food retail environment across areas and subpopulations. In general, high income meal client group can accept to choose to go to supermarkets or restaurants to spend than low income meal client group. The impact of the economic environment on sales of ready meals is such as an individual get richer, who can afford to buy ready prepared foods, rather than spend time and effort to prepare to cook them at home. It seemed that low income consumers were decreasing to eat meals at expensive restaurant to the alternative of relatively cheap ready prepared meals at home. Research could also consider how consumer knowledge and preferences and the time cost tradeoffs affect consumer decisions of which foods to eat and whether to make or to buy prepared foods from supermarkets or to eat at restaurant meals . Travel costs and time costs of acquiring foods as well as the time costs of preparing foods (meals) are also likely to affect demand for particular foods. Research on price variation at the local level and demand models could also be used to help determine which factors contribute to differences in access to food retailers. Price is also major determinant of food (meal) demand.

The higher, the price of a food(meal), the lower the meal quantity demanded. On the other hand, the higher the price of a substitute food (meal), the higher demand will be for that food (meal) item. Given the budget constraints of low income consumers and the price of some specific foods (meals), low income consumers may substitute higher priced foods (meals) with lower priced foods(e.g. hamburger for steak or canned fruits for fresh fruits). Considering restaurants foods purchasing choice, such as economies of scale, which is when the costs of operating a restaurant decreases as restaurant size increases and economies of scope, which is when the costs decrease as more meals variety increases, suggests that larger restaurants that offer greater variety can offer lower meal prices. Both factors may account for the ability of larger restaurants to survive more easily than smaller restaurants. Considering supermarkets foods purchasing choice, it is possible that food retailers (supermarkets) actually have some market power, especially in setting where there are few competitors to close. It would have an incentive to increase food (ready meal) price and restrict foods(ready meals) supply quantities to increase profit. Supply side conditions, such as economies of scale, it could lead to (ready meal) food retailers (supermarkets) to have more market power, if it was not close between supermarkets. Individual behavior to make healthy choices can occur only in a supportive economic environment with accessible and affordable healthy food choices. Hence, food environment and sale strategies is needed to consider to adopt the exported countries' economic change.

Food marketing client target groups can include home parents, students and working people groups mainly and marketing and economic environment factors would cause food choices and these factors impact health and nutrition and the focus on the connections between people and their environments.

In conclusion, macro level economic environmental factors play a more indirect role but have a substantial and powerful effect on what people eat. Macro level factors operate within the larger society, include food marketing, social norms, food production and distribution systems, agriculture policies and economic price structures as well as social environmental to influence within the home, such as model of healthful dietary intake by parents feeding style, frequent family meals may promote healthful food consumption among children.

CHAPTER TWELVE

online shopping sale price raising strategy

E-commerce how influences consumer behavioral changes to bring positive or better economy growth to the country?

I shall explain how e-commerce consumer behavior influences the country's economic growth or recession, they have direct case and effect relationship as below:

How can consumer e-commerce consumption behavior bring the economic impact of e-commerce ? E-commerce has altered the practice, timing, and technology of B2B and B2C markets, affecting everything from transportation patterns to consumer behavior. The development of electronic commerce, the most basic of economic transactions— the buying and selling of goods—continues to undergo changes that will have a profound impact on the way companies manage their supply chains. Simply put, e-commerce has altered the practice, timing, and technology of business-to-business (B2B) and business-to-consumer (B2C) commerce. It has affected pricing, product availability, transportation patterns, and consumer behavior in developed economies worldwide.

B2B e-commerce leads the way

Business-to-business electronic commerce accounts for the vast majority of total e-commerce sales and plays a leading role in global supply chain networks . In 2003, approximately 21 percent of manufacturing sales and 14.6 percent of wholesale sales in the United States were e-commerce related; by 2008 those percentages had increased to almost 40 percent for manufacturing and 16.3 percent for wholesale trade. One reason why B2B e-commerce is more sophisticated and larger in size than direct to- consumer e-commerce is that B2B transactions developed out of the electronic data interchange (EDI) networks of the 1970s and 1980s.

The steady growth in business-to-business e-commerce has changed the cost and profit picture for companies worldwide. At the microeconomic level, growth of B2B e-commerce results in a substantial reduction in transaction costs, improved supply chain management, and reduced costs for domestic and global sourcing. At the macroeconomic level, strong growth of B2B e-commerce places downward pressure on inflation and increases productivity, profit margins, and competitiveness.

Double-digit growth for B2C

E-commerce retail has become the fastest growing trade sector and has outpaced every other trade and manufacturing sector since 1999, when the U.S. Census Bureau started collecting and publishing data on e-commerce. That year, e-commerce retail sales represented less than 1 percent of total U.S. retail sales. In 2003 that number climbed to a little less than 2 percent; by 2008 it had grown to 3.6 percent, and by the fourth quarter of 2010 B2C e-commerce reached 4.4 percent of total U.S. retail sales. In dollar terms, e-commerce retail revenue currently stands at approximately US $165 billion, considerably less than the US $3.9 trillion that represents the total U.S. retail market.

During the "Great Recession," which lasted from December 2007 through June 2009, manufacturing, wholesale, and bricks-and-mortar retail sales took a heavy beating. By the fourth quarter of 2010 they still had not fully recovered, even though U.S. gross domestic product (GDP) and personal spending (adjusted for inflation) had surpassed their previous peaks seen in late 2007.

Retail e-commerce, by contrast, weathered the recession relatively well, albeit with considerably slower growth than had been seen prior to the financial crisis. In the first quarter of 2002, retail ecommerce experienced quarterly, year-over-year growth of about 42 percent. On the eve of the recession, that rate dropped to a still-respectable 18 percent. Quarterly sales continued to grow until the latter part of 2008, and in the fourth quarter of 2009 sales surpassed the previous peak

It's important to note here that a large portion of B2C sales come through mail-order houses, many of which have an online presence as well as traditional storefront outlets. Contrary to popular opinion, mail-order houses still have a very strong online presence, and until just recently their sales outperformed online-only retailers.

How e-commerce influence the country's economic and consumer

behavioral changes ?
The changes that B2C e-commerce has sparked arguably have had a more significant impact on the economy and on buyers' behavior than has B2B ecommerce. In the past, when consumers wanted to make purchases they had to set aside time to shop during certain hours of the day, or they had to read through catalogs sent to them by mail-order houses. Today, many consumers can simply use their computers— and now smart phones or other portable electronic devices—to shop online. Buyers and sellers that engage in e-commerce retail trade are no longer restricted by store hours, geographic marketing areas, or catalog mailing lists. With a few simple clicks they can gain access to a variety of goods 24 hours a day, seven days a week.

The characteristics of retail e-commerce merchandise also have changed significantly over the past decade. Back in 2000, computer hardware was the most common type of merchandise sold over the Internet. Today, the variety of merchandise is extremely diverse, and shoppers can buy almost anything online.

Online shoppers have benefited in other ways. The growth of e-commerce retail sales has reduced consumers' search cost, placed downward pressure on many consumer prices, and reduced price dispersion for many consumer goods. But this has led to a substantial decrease in the number of small companies operating in certain industries, as they tend to be less involved with e-commerce. Larger businesses, most notably retail book outlets, new automobile dealerships, and travel agents, are better able to compete in this new market environment.

The extremely rapid growth of e-commerce retail sales has provided a major boost to residential parcel delivery services. That's because online merchandise purchases involve some form of residential delivery by a third-party vendor such as FedEx, UPS, or the U.S. Postal Service. In addition, there appear to be considerable synergies related to B2C parcel and heavier freight volumes—parcel industry insiders have observed that businesses with strong e-commerce related B2C parcel shipment volumes often have stronger B2B shipment volumes than those that do not engage in B2C e-commerce.

How the E-commerce influences demand patterns ?

As technology, e-commerce, and globalization become more intertwined, buyers and sellers are increasing their connectivity and the speed with which they conduct sales transactions. As we saw during the recent turmoil in the financial markets and some supply chain networks, speeding up sales transactions can be a very positive attribute when small market corrections are taking place. However, during a major economic correction like the one we witnessed during the Great Recession, a quicker response to sales transactions can have cascading impacts on supply chains, resulting in large contractions or expansions in orders, production, shipments, and inventory. Thus, there are some potentially negative consequences to the rapid growth of e-commerce. In this volatile business environment, supply chain managers should consider developing strategies for dealing with the rapid swings that can result from increasing use of e-commerce in a globalized market.

In conclusion, the high technological e-commerce online shopping model change, it can influence consumer behavior change to influence any country's economic environment to change to be better or worse. So, they has direct relationship between the country e-commerce development and its economic recession or growth. The impact of e-commerce and R&D and two other variables on economy development in 21 selected countries. This study used panel data technique with Generalized Least Square Regression (GLS) method during the period of 2005 to 2013. The results showed that e-commerce and R&D had a positive and significant impact on GDP (Gross Domestic Product) per capita based on purchasing power parity, with e-commerce having a stronger development-enhancing effect in comparison to R&D. Health expenditure and government size as other dependent variables also had a positive influence on GDP per capita, which could be effective in improving and growing the economy.

REFERENCE

Biswas, D. (2009). The effects of option framing on consumer choices: Making decisions in rational vs. experiential processing modes. Journal of Consumer Behaviour, 8, 284-299.

Factors Influencing E-Commerce Development Implications for the Developing Country consumer behavior ?

The availability and continued growth of Internet technologies (IT) have created great opportunities for users all over the globe to benefit from IT services and use them in a variety of different ways. The use of IT to conduct business online is known as Electronic Commerce (E-Commerce). We are witnessing a boom of new technologies, especially in the service sector (IT, Telecommunications, Internet, etc.). Due to technological advances economic transactions have become much easier and faster and this is mainly because of the development of e-commerce. Real engine of the new economy, e-commerce is a remarkable source of competitive advantage for businesses and a new space for consumers. In the coming years, growth and profitability will depend most likely the ability to introduce these new emerging technologies and adopt new methods of business transactions. Since many years ago computers, appliances, plane tickets and many other items are available for purchase on the Internet using cards issued by local banks. Although this technological trend could significantly strengthen the national economic structure, its role and place in developing countries economic structure remains unclear and leaves many questions to ask:

Why does consumers need e-commerce in developing countries? What are the obstacles to e-commerce? Is e-commerce having a bright future to become a mainstream business for growth, and what steps to take to get there?

While developed countries have harnessed and adopted E-Commerce, developing countries are not yet fully adapted to its adoption. The aim of this study is to investigate the factors that play a role in the adoption and development of E-Commerce and, hence, develop strategies that conceptualize the influential factors that form as enablers and disablers of E-Commerce. In this paper we provide some answers about the current situation of e-commerce think later on prospects that will enable the benefits from all the advantages offered by this new mode of trade. This paper is organized as follows. Firstly, a concept of e-commerce is briefly introduced, followed by the construction of the research model, including all the aspects of e-commerce that are the object of our investigation. Finally, implications drawn on the study results and analysis are discussed, followed by the research limitations and a conclusion. factors influencing e-commerce. The factor may include as below to influence developing countries customer behavioral change :

● Security, Fraud and Hacking factor

It is widely acknowledged by both government and industrial organizations that, from a consumer point of view, issues of information security are a major obstacle to the growth of E-Commerce. The perception of risk regarding Internet security has also been recognized as a concern for both experienced and inexperienced users of Internet technologies (Miyazaki and Fernandez, 2001). Security and privacy: the perception of e-commerce portals as secure platforms without any uncertainty and adverse consequences after e-commerce use, and the ability to determine when and what extent information about them is communicated to others for maintaining confidentiality.

- Trust and Loyalty factor

The willingness of people to rely on and willingness to frequently use e-commerce portals for conducting transactions based on the feelings of confidence and assurance.

How to predict Consumer Behavior in the Retail Industry ?

Here is a not-so-rare scenario in retail. A sales promotion campaign has run for 3 years with loads of success, but then it fails in the 4th year. In most cases, there will be some amount of introspection to see what has changed in the company, and why the performance targets were not achieved.

In most cases, the change in consumer behavior is not caused by the company's branding efforts, but rather by external factors such as convergence of digital channels, analytics, changing customer preferences and most importantly the competition.

Allowances can be made for small changes in consumer behavior through past sales analysis and forecasting and by effective prediction of consumer demand. As rightly said by Steve Jobs, "customers don't know what they want until we've shown them." Retailers, must know what the customer wants, before the customer can know themselves. I shall recommend some ways to predict consumer behavior in retail industry as below:

Here are 5 methods that companies can use to predict consumer behavior:

1. Listen to your customer

After becoming the CEO of the ailing Procter & Gamble in 2000, A.G. Lafley had a simple mantra to revive his company, which was "The consumer is the boss." Reiterating this mantra to his employees, Lafley urged them to listen to what the consumers were saying and what they wanted from the products, especially when they are unable to articulate their needs. P&G was able to drive their business decisions, based on a complete understanding of the customer wants.

In another case in 2009, the makers of the Wrangler and Lee jeans generated an additional $100 million in revenue, simply by changing the size labelling of their jeans and promoting a campaign to help women find the right fit irrespective of their body size.

2. Improving sales forecasts

Applying forecasting techniques to sales and business decisions can help companies predict consumer behaviour. Use relevant data that focusses on the factors impacting the retail business industry, such as consumer sentiment, available credit, employment factors, and wages. Relevant indicators of future sales can help project the likely consumer behaviour. For example, drop in hourly earnings is an indicator of a likely drop in retail sales. Forecasting must also be applied to real business decisions. Be it marketing, staffing, or manufacturing decisions, accurate forecasting can help companies prepare for market opportunities by identifying potential growth markets and product lines.

3. Use of Predictive Analytics for consumer prediction
Predicting consumer behavior patterns based on customer interactions and transactions is extremely important in the digital era. Customer Experience analytics, Consumption based, spend analytics, Channel analytics or through digital footprints created by the user's web browsing can be vital predictor data for driving insightful engagements in retail.

4. Target non-buying customers
In addition to predicting buying behaviors of existing customers, companies must also pay importance on how to make their products valuable for non-buying customers. Providing a solution for customers whose needs were not addressed previously, can open a wide and untapped market for retailers.

5. Create product promoters
According to the consultancy firm, Bain & company, consumer satisfaction and market share are not the right predictors for consumer behaviour. Customer responses to simple feedback questions such as, "How likely are you to recommend this product to your friend?" on a scale rating of 1-10 is likely to produce more accurate results. Product promoters with a rating of 9 or more, can be used as reliable sources of buying patterns. Retailers need to develop a deeper understanding of these promoters, and also on how to convert more customers into promoters.

Insights Driven Sales is same to Customer Satisfaction
As clearly outlined by Lafley, retail businesses must clearly focus on the customer, and study the behavioral analytics of their customers. Customer Intelligence (CI), which is the process of gathering and analyzing data about customers, is clearly the need of the day. Such customer insights can help a business make a rational decision of their marketing efforts and product offering.

(6) What are Implications for Ecommerce in Developing Countries consumer shopping convenient need factor ?

In developing countries, IT and communication or rather e-commerce growth are substantial. Technology effectiveness is essential in E-Commerce success. However, human, economic, and other organizational issues must be taken into account as well. In this study, we evaluated the current status of E-Commerce in Developing countries. The evaluation of current status reveals opportunities that should be seriously tackled by organizations, if they are to survive the consequences of globalization and open markets. There should be an immediate implementation of a governmental infrastructure to support e-commerce. This thesis explored the areas enabling and huddles to the development of e-commerce. Online consumers face problems concerning security and privacy. They are exposed with online risk such as hacker mischiefs. Moreover, when buyers make payment using credit cards, they are exposing their banking information which could also be manipulated by hackers. The results of this research showed that majority of the respondents felt that internet shopping is risky due to the same reason. Amongst the perceived risks is financial, product performance, social, psychological and time convenience loss. Other than stolen credit card information, there are also risks in delivery. The time taken for delivery may take quite some time, therefore, anything could happen in the process of delivery. Buyers may lose the item. Online vendors might not be responsible for the loss and this leaves the buyers to bear all the consequence. When the perceived risk is greater, the relationship between intention and online purchasing will be weakened.

● Accessibility and Awareness factor

The perception of user interface quality and the degree of awareness on information about products and services delivered from conducting transactions from any location at any time through e-commerce portals. factors

● Quality and benefits factor

The perception of quality of products and services offered from e-commerce portals and benefits that arose from conducting such transactions.

In conclusion, Countries need to encourage and improve the e-commerce developments. This research sheds light on the potential factors that may play a significant role in supporting the proliferation and advancement of E-Commerce in developing countries. The outcomes of this study may contribute to the market stakeholders' understanding of their potential customers' needs and current concerns. Exploring the market, especially at this time while e-commerce is still in its development stage, is critical for industry stakeholders in order to ensure the success of this emerging market. Future research should focus on studying the development of e-commerce and testing the research model. Consequently, potentially important dimensions of the study could include an investigation in multiple cities, and especially in more rural areas, which may lead to more accurate and comprehensive results and analysis. Also, comparative research in different parts of the world would produce more complete findings. The results of this study could then be compared with those of other developing countries having similar conditions to see if there is a significant difference.

Reference

?Miyazaki, A. D., & Fernandez, A. (2000). Internet privacy and security: An examination of online retailer disclosures. Journal of Public Policy & Marketing, 19(1), 54-61, CrossRef

What are the negative influences or impacts to influence the country's consumer behaviors when the country is encountering any kinds of death disease ? Why does death disease bring economic recession to the country when the country can not control the death disease to cause many people to die , when they are free to go to anywhere and the owning death disease people can contract any people , they have no death disease easily?

What is the negative consumer behavior when the country has many people , they are owning death disease? Why can death disease bring economic recession to the country when it has many people are owning death disease risk?

The economic problem – sometimes called the basic or central economic problem – asserts that an economy's finite resources are insufficient to satisfy all human wants and needs. Economics involves the study of how to allocate resources in conditions of scarcity However, viewing economics as the study of how society allocates resources can lead to conflation of normative economic planning and empirical study of how economic agents operate in these conditions.

Such as one country has many people are owning death disease, there are many people feel unsafe, they will not dislike to go to any where because they are fear to be contracted from the owning death disease people, but they do not know whom are owning death disease. So, the restaurants, cinemas, shopping centers, libraries transportation tools etc. any public shopping or leisure places will have less people. When the country believe that any one will be contracted to get death disease easily and the government send this death disease message to let itself country to know that they will have death disease risk when they go to anywhere to contract any people, any the kind of death disease can pass air or mouth or hand contact method to cause the health people to get the kind of death disease from the owning death disease people. Then, many health people won't choose to go to anywhere to consume or play leisure easily because they are fear to get death disease from any death disease people in streets or public shopping centers or public libraries, book shops or cinemas or restaurants. So, it seems that death disease can influence consumers' purchase desires to decrease because they reduce time to go to any public places, e.g. shopping centers, entertainment places, streets, libraries, restaurants etc. places. So, restaurants will reduce eatting people number, cinemas will reduce audiences number, buses , taxi, ferry, trains, trams etc. public transportation tools will reduces passengers number. It seems that when the country is encountering death disease will influence consumers shopping desires to be poor because they dislike to go to anywhere easily.

So in supply and demand view, when the country is encountering serious death disease attacks, there are many shopping centers will lose customers, restaurants and cinemas , etc. business shops will reduce many passengers or eatting people or purchasers number suddenly in short time, e.g. one to three month, even in long time, e.g. above year. When the country is encountering death disease, many consumers' purchase desires will reduce (demand of purchase desires will decrease) , due to they are reducing time to visit any shops, go to cinemas, go to food shops , catch any public transportation tools to go to anywhere , because they are fear to contact the owning death disease people to get their death diseases by air, mouth or hand contract any time easily. In economic supply and demand theory indicates that supply number will either decrease or decrease price when demand is decreased. In this death disease suitation, many businesses will lose customers, when they are reducing time to go to anywhere as well as demand is decreased. Consequently, the owning death disease country businesses will attempt to reduce price much or reduce products supply number in order to attract many people choose to buy their products in the encountering death disease time. So, it seems that when one country is encountering death disease, the death disease will bring negative consumer emotion to influence the country's businesses or purchase demand. Unless, essential products, they won't be influenced to reduce demand when they country is encountering death disease, e.g. food, drinking water, medicine. So, hospitals, medicine shops, supermarkets, food stores , theses essential product sale shops their customers numebr will not be influenced to reduce easily when the country is encountering death disease. Hence, when one country is encountering death disease, it is not absolute that all businesses will lose many customers. Whether the shop will lose many customers, it depends on whether what products it is selling, if it sells essential foods or medicines, then I believe that its customers number will not be influenced to reduce due to the country itself is encountering death disease occurrence.

In mainstream neoclassical economics, it is assumed that humans pursue their self-interest, and that the market mechanism best satisfies the various wants different individuals might have. These wants are often divided into individual wants (which depend on the individual's preferences and purchasing power parity) and collective wants (which are the wants of entire groups of people). Things such as food and clothing can be classified as either wants or needs, depending on what type and how often a good is requested. However, when the country is encountering death disease occurence, food or medicine needs or demand won't reduce, even increases because many people are fear food shortage is caused or medicine shortage is caused due to death diseases causes food suppliers decrease food supply or medicine suppliers decrease supply to achieve their prices rise to earn more profit in the moment or many people decide to buy more food or medicine in the death disease occurrence time. So, it explains that why food or medicine prices will increase rapidly in the death disease occurrence time. Otherwise, restaurants, cinemas, any product sale shops will decide to reduce price much becuase their products or leisures are not essential to anyone. Anyone do not want to go to these places to avoid to get death disease from the owning death disease people's bodies contact, mouth contact , air contact channels easily.

However, economists have sometimes characterized "how" to produce as a "technological problem" of efficiency whereas the allocation of what is produced is an "economic problem". In a free market, the "how" of production and allocation of resources is distributed among economic agents. In a centrally planned economy, a principal decides how and what to produce on behalf of agents. Modern economies are often welfare capitalist with various regulations, which makes the economic system more equitable while retaining the distributed free market system. Due to human wants are unlimited, an infinite series of human wants remains continue with human life. Nobody can claim that all of his wants have been satisfied and he has no need to satisfy any further want. Everybody feels hunger at a time then other he needs water. Sometime one feels the desire of clothing then starts to feel the desire of having good conveyance. When all existing wants are satisfied then new wants starts to create in mind, so the series of wants remains continue till the last moment of life. So an economic problem arises because of existence of unlimited human wants.

However, in this death disease encountering country case, this country's people's unlimited human wants or unlimited consumer desires , e.g. enjoyable desires, comfortable desires will reduce. For example, cinema will reduce audiences number , although the movie is attractive to persuade many audiences to go to cinemas to watch, but due to many audiences are fear to enter any cinemas to contact the owning death diseases peoples' bodies, hands, air, mouth in cinemas easily. So, cinemas will not have many audiences when the country is encountering death disease occurrence time. For another example, car shops won't have many people to visit when the country is encountering death disease time. When one person hopes to visit any car shops to choose one car , he feels it is comfortable to drive before the death disease does not occur, but when the country government notifies there has first death disease personal contact case occurs from television or radio channel suddenly in itself country, then this cause will cause many people feel fear to go to anywhere easily. This bad news will influence the car desire buyer changes his car purchase to avoid to visit any car shops because he is fear to contact the owning death disease or illness patients when he neglects to contact any one whom are owning the death diseases on streets, from public transport tools, even when he enters the car shop to contact the salespeople , if it is unlucky, he contract the salesperson , he is owning death disease, when the saleperson and him, they are talking by mouth, then the owning death disease salesperson his dirty air will enter the car buyer's mouth from air channel easily. Then, he will be another owning death disease patient. So, enjoyable driving feeling will bring lose or decrease to this car desire buyer when the death disease is occurring in this country. So, it explains that why the enjoyable leisure consumers number must be decrease when the country is encountering death disease in the time.

However, when the country is encountering serious death disease to cause many people death time. Economic growth must be difficult to achieve, even recession is caused by death disease easily because many people avoid to spend time to leave themselves homes to go to anywhere to get this kind of death disease by air, bodies contact to others and mouth or any public places doors channel easily. In fact, consumers' demand will reduce because many people are fear to leave themselves homes when death disease occurs to cause anyone die in the country. So, it means that scarcity problem won't occur to the country when it is encountering death disease occurs. Unlimited wants will reduce or unlimited purchase desires will reduce or loss because people won't lose purchase desire , such as car buyer case. They won't leave themselves homes easily when they feel that they will get the death disease if they leave themselves homes. Also limited resources will not increase when the country is encountering death disease occurs because any products won't be sold easily. Hence, scarcity problems won't happen easily when the country is encountering death disease in the time. Unless, when the country has none any one is killed by the death disease, then many people will not feel fear to leave their homes to go to anywhere easily.

CHAPTER THIRTEEN

University school fee raising strategy

How can University campus location factor influence student choice?

University can attempt to predict student individual psychological needs to avoid student turnover numbers increasing. Whether University location can be a competitive advantage to attract students to study? The school (university) location means that the proximity of city center and the proximity of students home. To increase the occupancy rate, the university location is needed to provide as a model and resources based view which will be used to explain why the school location is a kind of competitive advantage for universities. According to Porter theory, it is a part of factor, which has some advantages against the treat of entry. It can decrease the treatment of rivalry. However, a good place has a certainly positive effect for attracting staff and more students. For resource-based view, the location is one of the internal resources for long term economic benefit production of factor. It can be accepted as one of the physical and tangible resource of a university.

I shall apply the first attractive factor of Porter five forces and resource based model to analyze my opinion to explain why school (university location) can influence students to choose the university to study. This view is represented by the opportunities and the threats. The university of thought is the resource based view which is represented by the strengths and weaknesses of the firm. Porter's five force model of competition elements include threats of entrants or substitutes, bargaining power of buyers or suppliers and competition rivalry. A firm's resources include brand name, in-house knowledge of technology, employment of skilled personnel, trade contract, machinery, efficient procedures and capital etc. Such as, both tangible and intangible assets are considered a firm's resources. For a university, customers can be thought as a students, suppliers can be thought as staff. In higher education industry, the good transportation infrastructure and well-connected universities have some advantages against the treat of entry to attract good staff and more students. The place of a university can decrease of treatment of rival and a good place has certainty positive location is an opportunity for universities to attract the students.

- The resource based theory of university
location competitive advantage

According to the Porter's theory, the resource based theory can apply competitive resources to be identifies to higher education institutions. For higher education institutions, such as resources might include the reputation of certain departments, the grouping together of areas of specialist expertise and the development of technical patents etc. Also higher education resources may not be imperfectly mobile, as the competitive resources of a university identifies tangible, intangible and organizational assets. So, the tangible resources might include campus location, building capacity, conference facilities and medical research facilities. Intangible resources generally include such items as patents, teaching and research performance, service levels and technology and the geographical location of a service. In a university, such intangible resources might include some of the above and may also include employees/ associates, e.g. experienced professors, renowned authors and distinguished teachers. Also, the location of a university can be accepted as physical and tangible resources of a university. However, I believe location is shown as an important factor to affect the students' university enrolment selection decisions.

To sources of competitive advantages are thought to be the reputation of the institution, the curriculum and educational standards, school fees (tuition), location and student activities etc. different factors. Moreover, any university's general client segments include such as, high school graduates, elderly students and international students, that have been influenced by several factors when selecting the best university to study. One of these factors is again location, the proximity to home and easy transportation is critical factor in selecting a university. Presumably, institutions that are located along well-established public transit routes have a competitive advantage over those with poor transit links. Due to the efficiency of innovation activity increased in easily accessible locations with a high density of economic activity. The existence of education and research institutions as well as easily available information is suggested as a reason for this increase. Also private higher education institutions desire to benefit from these flows by locating itself nearby. Therefore, together with other factors, such as existing capital global flows should be existing capital and population, level of income and location decisions of foundation universities. The location, social life campus, proximity of campus to the city center, exchange programs, the curricula infrastructure, languages medium of instruction and activities are the most significant factors to influence students to choose which university to study. By the past statistic indicated that the location has 94% rate, the proximity of campus to the city center has 84% rate. So, it seems the proximity of campus to the city center factor is more prior choice to compare with the school location is close to the student home factor.

Huang (2012) stated that " the right location attracts more students and ensures the revenues of the institution. The location of an educational institution might influence its future prospect of growth. A good location attracts not only more students, but also excellent teaching staff". Because of job opportunities areas, the students are able to get a part-time job and earn extra money for their tuition (Huang, 2012). Marketing concept has four "P", it can apply to university educational business, such as educational promotion, tuition price, teachers of people and school campus location of place.

Finally, I shall give two assumptions to explain why if the university location is not popular to be accepted to the country's students in general, then it will cause who won't choose to study the university. However, even if the university's tuition is reasonable or cheaper or lecturers are famous or reputation or educational advertisement is attractive. In fact, the poor location factor will influence many local or overseas students who don't choose to study the university in the country. The first assumption is that most of students feel that the proximity of the university to the city center factor affects their university final choice decision and the another assumption is that most of students feel that the proximity of university to home affects their university final choice decision. There two assumptions are used to determine the importance of university location to attract the students. In Porter theory, either proximity of city center and/or proximity of student's home of a university factors have same advantages against the treat of entry. It can decrease the treatment of rival and a good place has certainly positive effect to attract teaching staff and more students. In resource based view, the location can be accepted a kind of internal resources. It can be accepted as one of the sustainable competitive advantages literature, location is a kind of advantage for higher education institutions.

- The factor of student demand for alternative modes of course delivery

The factor of student demand for alternative modes of course delivery is another factor to influence the student who chooses the university to study. Any university's educational program includes program design, material production (both print and e-version), promotion, essay competition, school networks, budgeting, coordinating with various constructors, data base management and program evaluation etc.

Nowadays, university teaching methods may include face-to face, online and hybrid modes of course delivery. However, the several ways to students to deliver their course works ,such as full time, part time, internal/ non campus, external studies/distance education, summer school, winter school, semester study and trimester study. The multi site of a university , e.g. major provider of distance online education operates popular affordable learning for student to use internet to study. Although, students do not need to attend to university classroom to listen lecturer's teaching, but it can reduce face-to-face contact between lecturers and students in university classroom often.

Although, it is a technological and innovative and effective learning modalities. In fact, such new technological teaching modalities may be necessitated to the graduated or master degree or doctoral degree students. But, I feel the online teaching method is not suitable to the bachelor degree students. As the delivery of course content or the commoditization of knowledge must be re-thought to the bachelor's if the student can't enquire whose lecturer any questions to give feedback by face-to-face. Then, who will concern the course to feel more difficult possibly if who can't listen whose lecturer's opinion to solve whose challenges about the course any questions immediately in classroom often.

The second attractive factor of student demand for alternative modes of course delivery is another factor to influence the student who chooses the university to study. Nowadays, university teaching method include face to face, online and hybrid modes of course delivery. However, the several ways to students to deliver their coursework, such as full time, part time, internal/on campus, external studies/distance education, "summer school, winter school, semester study and trimester study." The multi site of a university, e.g. major popular provider of distance online education operates a flexible learning for student to use internet to study. It can reduce face to face contact between teachers and students into university classrooms. Although, it is a technological and innovative and effective learning modalities. In fact, such new technological teaching modalities may be necessitated to the graduated students or master degree or doctoral degree students. But, I feel the online teaching method is not suitable to the bachelor degree students. As the delivery of course content or the commoditization of knowledge must be re-thought to the bachelor degree students because whose knowledge level is limited if the student can't ask whose lecturer any questions by face to face contact. So, students will feel difficult to learn if who can't listen whose lecturers' teaching and to enquire any questions and to give feedback in classrooms immediately. It is possible that who will wait long time to ask many questions to prepare to wait lecturers to give feedback by email later if their lecturers use online teaching method. So it is essential that educators and administrators need to understand differentiated teaching demand to different knowledge level of students. Because student preferences may vary by age, cultural, background, degree types, learning style and matter etc. factors to decide whether whose students are suitable to teach by either online distance learning method between individual student and whose computer or face to face learning method between students and the lecturer in classroom face to face oral teaching educational method. In fact, working adults remain strongly associated eith interest in online delivery. However, the availability of evening/weekend choices is the second most important enrollment factor to adult students, due to who consider when enrolling in an institution to indicate the important of face-to-face traditional delivery at not convenient times. So, online education is most clearly suited to independent learners those individuals who are self-motivated and self reliant and those who have a problem solving orientation.

The 2006 year Eduventures survey found that students interested in associate, bachelor's and master's degrees were most open to whole online delivery, although who were also open to campus-based delivery. Similarly, Gartner's 2008 year e-learning survey found that complete graduate programs offered online continue online. For example, international student demand for Australian higher education is expected to exceed supply in 2020 year, and key 2025 year there will be a shortfall of 22,692 international places on projected demand of 290,848. There numbers imply that to meet demand, Australian universities may want to invest further in online degree/delivery options. However, recent statistics indicate dealing interest in fully online programs in South East Asia, and a survey of 469 transnational students in 2007 year found that a majority of students opposed online provision. These findings suggest that, when branch campuses are found to be prohibitively expensive, the future of transnational programs is in programs that include face-to-face interaction facilitated by an offshore partner of the educational provider. However, education consumers prefer to combine online delivery and geographical proximity. Some of students who are living close to university campus. So who can access to courses delivered in a traditional mode, but chose to take online courses for the flexibility to it afforded them. This is an increasing trend in U.S. institutions as well, whereas online courses are used to cater solely to non-traditional students at a long distance from the campus, increasingly such classes are made available to the mainstream student constituency.

Can online and hybrid courses will influence to university students to choose
the university to study?

How can the technology online teaching contributing improve student outcome? At least, learning outcomes for students in online and hybrid courses match those of students in traditional settings. When these are reasons to believe that the hybrid model would produce more effective learning outcomes than the fully-online model in theory. Also evidence suggests that e-learning continues to grow in popularity with the number of hybrid or blended courses increasing at the fastest rate, although online/ hybrid courses certainly do not outcomes courses presented the traditional (i.e. face-to-face traditional classroom) delivery method. These facts help to demonstrate that despite the popularity and increased availability of online courses. However, students still value traditional classroom methods and that online options may not significantly detract from on-campus enrollments.

Hybrid degree programs, also known as blended programs are courses of study that combine traditional classroom based instruction with significant amounts of online instruction, with each passing semester, hybrid degree programs become increasingly popular for students and universities alike.

Such courses allow students to reduce time-consuming trips to campus when still benefiting from face-to-face teaching method allow colleges and universities to more effectively use classroom space and to reduce cost. For these reasons, hybrid courses are often praised as the best of both classroom and online teaching methods, it is possible that students have chance to go to classroom to listen lecturer's teaching and who also have chance to use internet to learn from online teaching method as the same time. These is no standard model for hybrid education. Some programs may have students split their time evenly between online and on-campus instruction; some may have students complete the majority of their work online with occasional intensive weekends of on-campus activity and some require students to enroll in a combination of traditional classes as well as strictly online classes. Nowadays, a major educational consulting group found that hybrid or blended learning was the most rapidly growing delivery option when online, hybrid and traditional delivery options were taken into acount. Because of the trend towards more hybrid programming, university officials concern on their potential impact on enrollment levels for on-campus degree programs. Some speculate that hybrid programs have the potential to overtake traditional programs, when others hope to use hybrid programs as stepping stones to attract more students to campus on a full time basis. The structures of different programs reflect institutions' intent to use hybrid programs to attract students from non-traditional areas. For example, Michigam State university's Master of social work hybrid program accepts roughly 25 students per year. In 2008 year, these students lived anywhere from 85 to 435 miles from the main campus, therefore frequent in person activities were not feasible. Gather in addition to completing online assignments, students attended a one-week-summer institute on campus in June and face-to-face instruction sessions in smaller groups organized by geography once per month during the fall and spring semesters. In short, hybrid programs do not necessarily replace on-campus offerings, nor do they commonly draw more students to campus on a full time basis. Rather, they complement existing program offerings by reaching out to new packets of students who have the mean to visit campus on occasion but not regularly.

In conclusion, any university ought follow its subjects, student age, school location and tuition, lecturers' repuation and school research facilities etc. factors to decide whether the course is suitable to be chose either online teaching or face-to-face traditional classroom teaching or hybrid (online and face-to-face both) teaching method to teach whose different degree level students. Because these factors will influence who to choose which kind of subjects to study. For example, if many first year students feel the subjects are difficult to learn. It implies that online distance teaching or hybrid teaching method is not suitable to be taught to them. The traditional face-to-face contact traditional classroom teaching method is more suitable to be taught to them. So, it is flexible to any one of these teaching method to choose to teach any subjects to university student. It is no absolute suitable teaching method to teach any one of subject in any one of university. Because any university is independent, it means that the teaching method is suitable to be taught to the students in the university. It doesn't mean that the same teaching method is suitable to be taught to the students to another university because every university's lecturer's reputation, school tuition fee, course's contents and qualities and student age segment and location is different among of them. It is very difficult to ensure which kind of teaching method must be suitable to be taught to the subject to all universities in any countries. Thus, if the university can predict which student individual psychology needs, then it can reduce its student turnover number successfully.

CHAPTER FOURTEEN

Airport shopping sale price raising strategy

Can airport time consumption factor influence airport passenger shopping behavior ?

Instead of airport is one arrical and leaving terminal station place main function for any travelling passengers after the airplances had landed on the country airport's subway. I feel that airport has also another main functions. It can help the country to attract more travellers to choose to go to the country to travel as well as it can persuade them to raise consumption desire in their whole journeys after they leave the travelling country's airport if they feel the country airport's service performance can satisfy their short time staying need. I shall explain why any countries‘ airports can influence travellers' travelling destinations and travelling shopping choices to be increased or decreased.

The future airport will be the assistance role to assist tourim industry development. The factors include, for example, safety and terrorism control, when the travellers feel the country's airport is safe to stay when they catch air planes to arrive the coutry first time. Then, the country's airport can build safe image to let them to feel the country is safe to travel indirectly, traditional cirport service providers will need to seek new service way to deliver value, such as subscription based service models can let travellers to feel the country's airport can provide one comfortable and enjoyable short term travelling staying environment in the country's airport. Then, they bring pleasant emotion to prepare their journey trip after they leave the airport in the foreign country.

So, if the country's airport can let the travellers feel safe and comfortable , then it can bring new exciting and enjoyable feeling to the country's image. Because airport will be any travellers‘ first time arrival place after they catch airplanes to arrive another country. So, positive or negative airport's image will influence travellers how they feel whether the country , it is worth to choose to travel indirectly. However, airports need have good facilities to satisfy any related airplane service employees or any airport food or product businesses need, instead of travellers' need. For example, it needs have good allocation of terminals and access to facilities , they will be managed and regularly reviewed and regarded their good facility availability , capacity constraints and the best use of available facilities to satisfy any food or product sale shops' sale need and airport passengers' purchase need both in airports or airplane pilots, airplace service employees, irport security employees' comfortable working environment need.

However, airport inside and outside also needs to be arranged enough parking space facilities to let any aircraft parked or stored at the airport from the place where it is parked or stored in order to let any vehicles to be parked in airports or ouside airports easily and conveniently. When any sudden emergency matters occurred, the aircraft subjects to unforeseen operational delays , it should need to contact airport operations control centre to indicate when the expected time of arrival and departure is, there is no need to request a new slot in cases of unforeseen operational delays where the operation will take place within 24 hours of the agreed slot time. For example, of unforeseen operational delays include aircraft technical issues or weather conditions that could not have been planned for. Hence, operationally delayed aircraft must utilise slots in the same manner as originally agreed. If any change to the original slot agreement is required, e.g. a slot must be requested immediately. Moreover, when aircraft subjects to non-operational delays must request new slots immediately, following the correct process in those conditions of use, an example, of a non-operational delay may include delay caused by late running passengers or poor schedule planning. Hence, airport needs have good facilities and communication system to coordinate to any departments to avoid aircraft unforeseen delays to cause airport passengers feel nervous and brings negative and poor emotion to the airport's service performance.

On airport baggage handling function aspect, airport operators must comply with the baggage policy made available to all operators with the airline business management team. For example, where a flight destination or carrier is identified as being at significant or high risk, the operator will pay a charge as notified by management, equating to the cost of any policing cost additional to the services normally provided at the airport for carriers or destinations at lower levels of risk. In fact, airport baggage management needs be checked and delivered in order to help any airplanes' passengers to transport their baggages to follow their airplanes to be delivered to their same destinations when their airplanes are flying with the passengers and whom baggages to arrive the same country's airport at the same time absolutely. So, barrage management operators need submit or demand and in agreed format the already fleets absolutely, such as fleet detail to report these data to include aircraft type and registration, number of seats maximum take off weight kilogrammes of each aircraft owned or operated by the operator, in order to avoid any passengers' luggages wrong delivery occurrence in possible.

Hence, any airports must need to consider above basic passenger service operation in order to avoid any accident occurrences to bring poor airport service attitude feeling. If airport management expected that they have good service performance to satisfy travellers' short term staying needs in themselve countries' airport.

Any countries' airports expect to increase passenger movements, they must have effective strategies to carry on reviewing any errors and improve performance effectively. For instance, how to keep cost effective measures to lower operating costs and keep good performance on quality, such as for maintenance and cleaning airport cost reducing measures to introduce variable, performance -based elements to encourage productivity gains, how to manage and implement new technological systems to improve information flow and work processes within the country's airport, e.g. airport e-immigration system can allows to receive real-time alerts on any airport building faults. It can reduce airport reliance on manpower in these areas, thus reaulting in better productivity and cost savings for long term airport expenditure. So, high technological strategy system is needed to implement to any country's airport in order to facilitate the handling of more aircraft movements to optimise aircraft handling on runways. Their benefits include reduction of departure flights separation times, reconfiguration of flight routes, and improvements in runway inspection processes.

These new measures can bring effective in improving any country's airport's runway efficiency, developing new infrastructure including the extension of the taxiway, roadway and power supply networks. It aims to satisfy travellers' convenient transportation needs when they arrive any countries' airports and prepare to find suitable transportaton tools to arrive their destinations more easily (airport transportation roadway, taxiway building network strategy).

Hence, any countries' airports need have good strategy to manage a wide range of activities and risks, which are broadly classified into strategic , financial operational, regulatory and investment. Any countries' airports also need to seek how to reduce the occurrence of risks and to minimum potential adverse impact as much as possible, uch as airport risk management strategy. Because when the country has many people are living and they need often to catch airplanes to leave their countries to travel as well as there are many foreign travellers choose to travel the country. Then, the country's airport must need to expand size and raise good facilities, e.g. more automated immigration gantries are needed to be installed, taxi waiting areas are also needed to be explanded with additional taxi bays constructed to accommodate the higher number of arriving passengers , even increasing airplane subways number to satisfy many airplanes need to fly away from the country's airport or coming airplances fly to the country's airport's landing on runway needs often.

So, airplane subways number expanding strategy and cutomated immigration gate fast checking system is needed when the country has many travellers choose to go to the country travel and/or many local people need to leave themselves countries to travel. For instance, departure and arrival immigration control as well as pre-boarding security screening will be controlled for more efficient deployment of manpower and equipment. Moreover, in the line will the trend of self-service options of airports arrived the world, provisions will be made to have more kioslls for self check in,self-bag -tagging and self bad-drops. The increasing use of these options will help airlines and ground handling agents reduce processing times and staffing requirement. For example, a fully automated to reduce reliance on scare manpower baggage check in and check out system, the baggage handling system will also be equipped with ergonomic lifting aids to enable heavy and odd-sized bags to be handled with ease, even by older workers.

Then, the country's airport must need to increase subways number and immigration fast checking service facility to avoid handling passengers crowd queueing problem often occurs every day. When any airports often let passengers feel time pressure to queue to spend long time to wait immigration checks and leave the airport. It will bring their negative emotion feeling to the country's airport. Then, it is possible to influence they choose to go to the country to repeat travel again. Hence, the country's different airport strategies are needed when the country has increasing travellers number trend as soon as possible.

Another strategy concerns airport emergency service on safe aspect. Any countries' airports need have a highly trained specialist wait that is positioned to provid fast action rescue and fire protection for passengers' life safety ,e .g. aircraft rescue and fire fighting vehicles are needed airport. An incident command and control simulator which provides realistic and interactive simulations of emergency scenarios for the purpose of any sudden accident occurrences in any countries' airports.

So, any countries' airports need to develop an internal digital system to ease labour-intensive work processes like fire safety inspection, incident reporting, logistic management and recording of its personal fitness results, with the new safe system , data entry is needed mobile enabled with the use tablet computers. For example, the airport safe unit can continue to enhance its emergency preparedness and rescue capabilities with the successful staging of two drills, simulated aircraft crashes on land and at sea, as well as any exercises validated crisis contingency plans are recommended to earn strong capability in coordinating rescue efforts involving both the airport community and mutual aid agencies in order to carry on rescuing passengers and airport pilots and service attendants whom life safe service when air planes are crashed on land and at sea.

Another strategy is now aviation facilities strategy, it can support fly, cruise and fly-coach initatives, important options to a rising number of interm travellers, if it can be implemented successfully. It can bring enhancement measures benefits, includes the reduction of departure flight separation times, reconfiguring of flight routes and implementation of aircraft speed control for increased runway use efficiency.

Hence, one successful airport operation , the airport management needs to know how to implement the traveller check out or check in service functions when they arrive the airport or leave the airport and to satisfy its passengers' short term terminal station staying or transfering another airplane's flying need as well as it also needs to know how to implement its different strategies to improve its service performance and to let passengers have more confidence to the country's airport service operators' behavior and they also feel safe when they are staying the country's airport. Hence, any travellers' short term staying feeling in the country's airport , whether the country's airport can bring either positive or negative emotion , which will influence they choose to go to the country to travel again in possible. Hence, airport management can not neglect how to improve airport service performance to satisfy any first time or more time airport visitors' short term staying need.

Can the country's airport service performance influence passengers consumption desire?

Nowadays, travelling is a kind of popular entertainment whn working people have holidays, retired people have more savings and students need to go to holiday to feel rest time after they had hard to study. They will choose go to other countries to travel. So, " freguent travelling times" which will increase to any travelling consumers. If the traveller often chooses to go to the country to travel, he must need to permit to enter the country from its airport immigration. If his every visiting time to the country's airport, he feels the country's airports' staffs services are poor performance and he feels that they are not polite or rude attitude to treat him when he needs to check out or check in from the country's airport immigraton gates, even he feels difficult to enquire any airport service staffs, either he feels difficult to find them or they need to spend long time to let him to queue to wait enquiry, even he also needs to spend long time to queue to wait check in or check out in airport immigration gates when he arrives the country's airport or he leaves the country's airport.

All of these negative airport staffs' service attitudes and poor service behavioral feeling, they will cause the frequent traveller doubts whether the country is a worthy travelling place and it is possible to led his negative consumption desire in the country's airport. Then, all of these negative emotion will influence the frequent traveller reduces consumption in the country's airport , even wothut any consumption in the country's airport, when he visits the country to travel every time. So , it seems that airport's service performance will influence travellers carry on more or less consumption in the country's airport. Then, it will influence all the country's airport related retail and restaurant businesses' sales to be reduced indirectly in the country's airport.

Instead of airport service performance intangible factor aspect, the airport's clean, airport itself appearance attractive design, large size and shops and restaurants' suitable locations and internal environment design etc. these tangible factors will also influence travellers' consumption desires in the country's airport. For example, in one special day, e.g. Olympic Games day, the Olympic Games country's airport may complete in record time and its airport can successfully handle a estimate record 85,000 minimum departing passengers a day during the Olympic Games period, twice the number on normal days. Travellers and media will describe the Olympic Games country's airport retail shops and restaurants consumption experience as seamless, magical and unforgettale airport staying experience, if the Olympic games country's airport can provide an excellent service performance on the Olympic games period. Then, it will influence the increasing sale amount in the Olympic Games country airport retail stores and restaurants during period. So , when the country is experiencing special day, such as "Olympic Games " is chosen to carry on competition in the country. Then, in this Olympic Games period, it will attract many travellers to choose to go to this country to travel, due to they have interest to watch Olympic Games competition in this country. This country's airport will represent this country's image. If it 's airport service staffs can provide excellent service to let any one of travellers to feel when they are staying in this country's airport short time and this country's airport itself appearance and design can also be changed more attractive and beautiful and the airport's retail stores and restaurants also design more attractive and beautiful. Then, the travellers' consumption desires will be possible to raise , when they visit this country's airport in first time in this Olympic Games travelling period.

In the future, if the country has a strong and affordable global air transport network, it will bring more advantages. Due to many travellers expect to catch air planes which can fly to another country in short time , it can reduce accidents occurrence chance on sky or on sea. So, short time flying can be more attract to compare long time flying. So, it explains that why many travellers prefer to choose one way flying more than transfering another /other air plane(s) flying. Although, they need to pay more air ticket fee. So, if the country's airport can have more subways number and large subways areas to let many arrival air planes and leaving air planes need to fly from land or fly to land in the country's airport frequently. Then, the travellers can buy any air tickets to book same day or next day or later day flught time to fly to any country to travel more easily, when the country's airport has large area size and many subways to let many airplanes can stay in its aircraft subways in same time. Then, the country's airport flight frequency will increase , it means that there are many travellers can catch airplances to fly to other countries in any time very easily from themseleves country's airport. It is time-sensitive feeling to let the country's travellers, they can feel to fly to other countries to travel in short day. They do not need delay to fly to any countries, when the flight airline is either full seat or the time can not permit any air places land on the country's subways.

So, none delaying time sensitive travelling frequent flught model will be one attractive flight flying method to influence the country's travellers choose to frequent travelling behavior. Because they do not change their travelling day, due to airplanes have no enough seats supply or the country's airport has no enough land subways to let any airplanes to stay to cause delaying their flight travelling booking seat day expectly.

So, airport is similar to airline to need to use different customer relationship management to attract returning travelling customers . It brings this question: What are the most attractive motivation factors in airport travel market?

I believe that factors may include airport loyalty, various flight time arrangement distribution channel, passenger check in or check out, laggage safe delivery, airpor security service. Moreover, flight schedules are also a main factor influences the travellers' final travelling country choice decision among different travelling countries. However, if the country's airport can build good loyalty image when passengers are staying in the country's airport in short time, it can show a more attractive motivator to increase travellers' consumption desires when they are staying in the country's airport in short time.

Hence, airport 's loyalty seems have relationship to influence travellers' consumption behavior when they are staying in the country's airport. For example, when the different countries' travellers feel enjoyable and happy to stay in the country's airport longer time. Then, their airport long time staying behavior will raise their consumption desire and chance to find any right restaurant to eat food or drink or find any right retail shop to buy right products in airport. Hence , when the country's airport can buil loyal customers relationship. Then, it will bring the advantages or benefits to the airport's any retail shops or restaurants on sale growth aspect, such as : their retention rates will go up easier, their customer referrals will go up easier, the country airport retail shopd and restaurants travelling customers whom spending rates will go up easier, the country airport retail shops and restaurants customers will be loss price sensitive, the costs of retail and restaurant servicing then will go down easier. Hence, if the country's airport customer service performance can maximize travellers' loyalty. It will influence travellers to feel the country airport's retail shops and restaurants have more loyalty to compare other countries airports' retail shops and restaurants loyalty.

So, it implies that any any country airport's loyalty will have relationship to influence its travellers how they feel the country airport's retail shops and restaurants' loyalty. Due to loyalty is intangible and it is obly feeling. So, when the travellers have positive emotion and wheh they are staying in the country's airport long time. Then, they will have positive emotion to spend more time to walk around in the country's airport as well as when they are passing any airport's retail shops or restaurents. Their pleasant emotion may encourage their consumption behaviors to have interest to find any right restaurant to eat food or drink or find any right retail shop to buy any right product in the country's airport in preference easily. Because they had been accepted to spend long time to stay in the country's airport, when they feel interest and surprise to visit the country airport when they arrive. Moreover , the long airport staying time will increase their purchase chance to any the country's airport's retail stores or restaurants in the country 's airport in first time visiting.

When one country's airport can satisfy passengers expectation to accept its service demand, then profitability and passenger number will be influenced to increase. So, airport management needs to focus on how to satisfy any passenger individual need or expectation when he/she needs to stay in whose country's airport for wait to either transferinf another airplance need to carrying on check in or check out in the country's airport immigration gate need in short time.

However, because if the country's airport service can let its passengers feel happy , then they will be super spenders to spend airport staying longer time to consume or entertain in the country's airport. Moreover, it will bring any the country airport's retail shops or restaurante to earn more sale growth indirectly. So, any country airports need to consider how to bring excellent customer services for any passenger individual need in airport. Because its service behavior or performance will have indirect relationship to impact the county airport's any businesses and itself any parking , entertaining services income in airport.

" The concept of managing airport customer expectation on passenger service quality" will be any country airport's main aim. Basically, airport passengers' perception concern how the airport service staffs' service attitudes or performances influence how they feel either negative emotion, such as anger, dissatisfaction, irritation, neutrality or positive emotion, such as happy, satisfaction, pleasure, delight. So, when the airport passenger individual perception is better , then his expected to the country airport individual service staff level will be at the highest level, but if his service expectation is less than his expectation standard, then the airport passenger will dissatisfy with the lowest satisfaction level to be influenced the country airport's other any one service staff by the one airport service staff whose poor performance. Because any one of the country airport's service staff , every one will influence the country airport's image. Of every one has excellent service performance, then, it will let many different counties' passengers feel sympathetic emotion from their every one's behavior. Otherwise, if every one has or most service staffs have poor or not considerate ot not sympathetic service attitude to be let them to feel, then any one of them will let many itself airport's countries‘ passengers feel the country airport's image is poor. They won't like to spend long time to stay in the country airport, even their short time airport staying behaviors will influence the country airport's any retail shops or restaurants businesses sale growth to be reduced from their short staying time influence.

In general, airport service staffs need to spend some time to answer any passengers' enquiries. So, how they answer their enquiries will influence how their achievement in order to raise the country airport's passengers satisfactions. It may lead a rise in different countries‘passengers' loyalty and retention, therefore the country airport can increase many different countries passengers number when the repeating airport visitors , they prefer to choose to go to the country to travel again , due to its airport is attractive reason in possible.

So, any country airport management ought have a policy from how the airport established desirable standard performance, measure it against actual performance to action taken once and revise any unachieved acceptable service level to the acceptable excellent passenger service performance in the country airport. For example, any country airport needs to manage and identify the target passenger segmenation target groups and to make bettwe understand the key elements that have the greatest impact on meeting every different target passenger segmentation group individual expectations and needs from their services in themselves country airport. So, any country airport will have relationship to any one of airline, as well as any one airline will have direct relationship to every passenger when he/ she stays in the country airport in short time.

However, instead of restaurants and retail shops; sale relationship will be influenced by the country airport's service performance, airport management also bring more empahsis on non-aeronautical (non related airlined and retail business) revenues, such as shops rents, concessions, car parking service income, consultancy and property developed diversified service incomes. So, airports need to focus directly to enterainment travelling airlines' passengers, meeters, and greeters, business-travelling passengers , users of general aviation services and transfer air plane short time staying visitors, or lone time staying visitors, e.g. the passengers need to live airport hotel for on night or more than one night sleeping before they catch the airplane on the day. So, all these different target passenger segmentations will have different service needs in any country airports.

However, airport passengers' behaviors and expectations of the airport experience depend highly on the types of traveller, they include: demographic characteristics, (i.e. gender, age group, income, sex, occupation) , purpose of trip (i.e. leisure, business), and their circumstances. In general , the passenger can be divided into different group, such as arriving, departing and transfer with different expectation and need, in the way they will be using the airport services and facilities different need and will also influence the behavior of individuals when in the commercial area. For example, passengers who are departing and arriving will require all airport facilities including: car rental, rail, buses access, pre-booking taxi service, check in or check out service, bad processing and security check and vertical and horizontal moving in passenger terminals. Otherwise, transfer passengers will have a short waiting time in airport and their needs will be likely different from those of origin and destination passengers. Some of the transit passengers will need to spend one hour, even more than four hours or half day in the airport. By providing airport facilities that can accommodate their needs, such as a place to lie down and take a short sleep time, free shower, free email public service will mostly give than an enjoyable airport experience. Evem some handicapped people or old people who feel difficult to walk in the airport corridor. Then , the airport will need to arrange the auto -wheel chairs and auto airport vehicle facilities to let service staffs to provide electronic auto wheel chairs to let them to sit down or drive the auto airport vehicle to sit down with them to go to their destination in the airport's any places immediately. For passengers travelling with families may want children play areas, where kids can have a great time when waiting to board the aircraft.

They also want the availability of rooms of families travelling with badies equipped with changing facilities, baby crib, microwaved and hot water need. When passengers are on business trip, may want a lounge, with all the business, facilities that they can feel free to use, such as free internet access and other services , such as fax, scan and photocopy machine. Hence, any airport managements need to develop the strategic customer facilities providing service in order to improve the design and delivery of all the facilities and services need by understanding expectation of each passenger segmentation group in their airport staying time.

Finally , in airport unique design aspect, our global airports will need have different unique design to let any travellers to feel that the country's airport can have its unique design to let themm to feel the country airport has itself own airport culture or entertainment features to attract they observe its appearance in order to achieve the increase more travelling visitors number when they feel enjoy to stay in the country airport longer time before they leave the airport. I shall indicate different countries' airports how they will perform themselves different airport cultures and unique design as below:

For China and Hong Kong Chinese airport design example, their airports need have Chinese cultural feeling to let Western travellers to feel their airports' designs and cultures are different to any Western countries' other cultures. So, China anf Hong Kong airports' designs can increase many old big size building photos number in their airports to let foreign visitors can walk on the long glass walkway corridor , when they enter walkway coddidor to walk through different 100 more airplane leaving and arriving gates number and the ground floor is built from heavy glass material. So , any one foreign traveller need to walk through on the long glass walkway corridor to pass any one gates to arrive his/her airplane leaving and arriving gate location and catch airplance to fly. Also, the glass walkway ground floor can let them to see the airport's vehicles and airplanes and people and trees outside environment clearly when they are walking on the airports' all glass material manual made ground floor. It will let foreign travellers feel China and Hong Kong airports building designs are different to the foreign countries' themselves airports' designs as well as Hong Kong and China airports' old building photos will let all leaving passengers feel difficult to forget their old building historical photos and they will know hoe their architectural skills are developed to imprved to build nowadays unqiue desing method from traditional building design method in Hong Kong and China airports. Otherwise, for US, Uk etc. foreign countries their airports designs can increase underground floor fish pool architectural design outside to their airports in order to let any passengers feel that they can see many different kinds of various fishes are swimming. So, their outside large fish pool can let them to feel surprise when they are staying in their any airports, e.g. one beautiful large size fish pool, it can be built to close to their airports and the fish pool can have various kinds of big and small fishes swim in the pool to let passsngers to see, or their airports can appear suddenly and unexpected of a gaping hole in the airport's outside ground, known as a sinkhole. Sometimes, the airport's outside sinkhole will fill up with fresh water to become deep , shaped manual made sinkhole to let passengers to feel they need to enter to the sinkhole and then they can enter the airport. So, the outside large size sinkhole will attract many passengers to stat to observe how the fresh water is entering to the sinkhole interestingly. Then, they will feel surprise when they need to pass though the sinkhole , then they can enter the airport.

In conclusion, attractive airport architectural design will let any passengers can not forget that they had ever visit the country to travel in their travelling experience as well as they can be influenced to like to stay longer time in the country airport by the airport's attractive design and environment influence. The most important influnece, it can influence airport related business income when they like to stay longer time in the airport.

CHAPTER FIFTEEN

Disney ticket price increasing strategy

What strategy can solve long time queue to bring theme park entertainment industry visitors negative emotion ?

For theme park entertainment industry, when visitors enter to any entertainment theme park , they need to queue to wait long time to play any entertainment machine facilities, which will bring their negative emotions and it can influence they feel not choose to go to the entertainment theme park to play any entertainment machine facilites again. Then, it will be possible to reduce the entertainment theme park visitors number because they can choose another entertainment theme park to replace it. I shall indicate Walt Disney entertainment theme park case example to explain how it avoids visitors feel long time queue pressure to influence their positive entertainment emotion during they are staying in Disney.

In the past Disney background history, Disney had encountered human resource and strategic management etc. different challenges about ten years. How to design its entertainment facilities to attract many visitors to visit and let they feel no any queue time pressure when they have interest to play any entertainment facilities, due to global entertainment theme park competitors are increasing, how to change its image to let visitors to feel it has much different image to compete its competitors. I shall explain how and why Disney needs to arrange entertainment facilities management to avoid any visitors feel time pressure when they need to queue to play as below:

First, what is a tourist destination and space tourist destination difference? e.g. space trip routes, Disney trip routes. Because any Disney visitors can not play all entertainment facilities and visit any entertainment destination in one day as well as any space travellers can not catch the space ship to fly all routes in space in one day. Hence, any Disney entertainment theme park and space tourism companies need provide any suitable space tourism destinations or Disney entertainment facilities destinations to let consumers to choose to entertain.

A tourism destination has many different characteristics. It is one product but also many,involves many stakeholders with differing objectives and requirements, is both a physical entity and a socio-cultural one, is a mental concept for potential tourists, is subject to the influence of current events, natural disasters, terrorism, health scares etc.is subject to historical, real and fictitious events,

is evaluated subjectively in respect of its value-for-money (based on reality compared with expectations), and differs in size, physical attractions, infrastructure, benefits offered to visitors and degree of dependence on tourism ? In fact no two tourism destinations can be treated the same. Disney ought to choose space travel feactures to attract many visitors, so it ought no choose general earth tourism features because space tourism features are more attractive and fresh ideas to attract visitors, e.g. space toursim related entertainment facilities, space tourism 3 D to 5 D movies to provide visitors to watch to feel who are sitting in space flying boats to travel during they are staying Disney theme park any time. So, they will feel Disney theme park is one space tourism boat similarly.

Second, what are between space tourism impacts and Disney entertainment impacts difference ? Tourism has a far wider range of direct and indirect impacts than other economic sectors. At its simplest tourism can be seen to be a temporary addition to the population of a given location, with tourists having all the needs and impacts that the permanent population does, plus a few more besides. Government planning, regulation etc. is therefore needed; yet tourism is an economic sector executed by the private sector. Tourism activity involves direct contact with the local population. Tourism, then, involves a triumvirate of destination interests ?state, private sector and community.

As such, Disney must let visitors to feel that it can provide space tourism service to let they to play in short time , it is not general tourism servic to satisfy their space toursim entertinment theme park difference. Space tourism planning for development and marketing is unlike any other economic sector and requires special approaches, procedures and institutions. Thus, Disney needs to know that space tourism features are different to general earth tourism as well as what factors will influence whose consumers do not choose to find their entertainment service. e.g. expensive air ticket, too cold or too hot weather, expensive space ship tickets or Disney admission fee , crowd in Disney or space ship etc. different factors to influence whose customers‘ choices.

Third, what is the difference between general earth tourism and space travel tourism perception? ?what is reality? How between space and earth tourism difference between a destination, or commercial tourism organisation, promotes its products and/or services is a key factor in the realisation of developmental or economic/financial objectives. In an activity like earth tourism where the customer is so far to live from the place he/she is considering to visit. Otherwise, on space tourism perception and reality hand, such as spending long time to catch plan to arrive Disney or space ship destination or what entertainment service he/she is thinking to buy, such as Disney entertainment facilities or space ships facilities. Disney space entertainment tourism marketing is a central component of tourism. Two of the adages of tourism marketing arising from this situation are that:

(1) Disney cannot test drive a earth holiday only? and it ought let its visitors to feel space tourism hoilday in short time enjoyable entertainment feel, such as they can feel that they are sitting rockets to fly to moon to travel in short time.

(2) On Disney short time space tourism, the perception is the reality to its visitors' space tourism feeling in short time?

Disney long time wait queue pressure problem

Wiig, k.(1993) indicated that The Walt Disney Company is one of the largest media and entertainment corporation in the world. Founded on Oct. 16, 1923 by brothers Walt and Roy Disney as a small animation studio. Today, it is one of the largest Hollywood Studios and also owns eleven theme parks, two water parks and several television networks, including the American broadcasting company. Disney entertainment theme park expansion has in recent years focused heavily on Asia, and specifically China, Hong Kong, Japan.

What factors caused Walt Disney strategic and human resource problems ?

In the beginning, Disney underestimated and neglected some strategic and organizational behavior issues which can influence its different departments‘ operations inefficiently. What factors caused Walt Disney human resource and hotel operational problems?

On the human resource problem hand, Bahandin, G et al., (2009) indicated that" errors are made regarding overall operation for Euro Disneyland from its American experience that Disney throughout Monday would be the light day for guests and Friday would be a heavy day to allocate staffs. In fact to this day, it had not enough staff to supply to staffing at a theme park, where the number of visitors per day in the high season can be 10 times the number in the low season ; wrong operational assumption of bus driver, it built the French bus parking space much too small. Bus drivers were unhappy as they had a very difficult time fitting their buses into their designated spots. In addition, Disney provided only 50 restroom facilities for bus drivers and on peak days there would be 2000 drivers ; operational errors are made to computer involved stations at the hotels. It assumed guests would stay at the park for morning spent the day at the park checked into the hotel late that night, and then checked out early the next morning before heading back to the park. Since there were so many guests checking in and checking out, additional computer station had to be installed at the hotels in order to decrease the amount of time the guests stood in line and hotel counter service staff numbers would also need to be increased. "

On the hotel operation problem hand, Dickson et al.,(2005) also indicated that" it had wrong belief that it understood European breakfast taste and Disney was told Europeans didn't eat sit down breakfast. This resulted in Disney downsizing their restaurants before Euro Disneyland opened. In fact, they were trying serve 2500 breakfasts in a 350 seat restaurant at some of the hotels. Further guests wanted bacon and eggs rather than just coffee. Disney reacted quickly with pre-packaged breakfast delivered to rooms and satellite. Thus, it caused result in Disney downsizing their restaurants."

The reasons showed that French Disney restaurants are caused to fail , such as lacked French cultural characteristics, but only European social and eating pattern ; the non availability of alcohol proved, employees were not expected to be spoken in French language and who also were not fluent in English. Hence, Disney restaurants can not accept French eating style and culture to attract many French visitors to go to Disney restaurants to eat. Due to, USA Disney did not follow French people eating taste and speaking cultural, It must cause its French restaurant operation unsuccessfully before.

In addition, Disney has wrong judgement to operate its business in USA and overseas Disney operation wrongly. Such as Disney estimated the demand of employee numbers wrongly. It only employed an additional 200 experienced Disney managers were located in the other three centres. In addition, some 4000 employees were unable to find suitable positions. It caused management lacks optimistic assumptions to know who ought to be provided training to its staffing to dealt cultural difference challenges. Moreover, it also had external threats and internal weakness challenges. It included high bank investment interest rates charge , unreasonable working conditions, poor communication and lack of cultural awareness because managers and it caused staff turnover increasing finally. The most failure, before Disney had not carrying on research whether whose visitors feel happy and satisfactory to enjoy its entertainment facilities when who are staying in Disney. Otherwise, who feel unsatisfactory and unhappy , even who need to complaint whose service quality. Hence, Disney numbers of visitors was decreasing before. Such as, visitors felt unhappy because who need to spent much time to queue. It also caused Disney visitor numbers was declining. Thus, Disney will need to consider how to change human resource activities to adapt clients' needs, such as reducing bad emotion to cause visitors who needed to spend much time to queue to wait to play entertainment facilities.

Disney traditional knowledge management strategy

Disney had attempted this traditional knowledge management strategy to solve its human resource and daily business operation challenges successfully. As Harriet Griffey (2010) stated that "sometimes, boredom can give disadvantages to reduce staffs' ability to motive to work and reduces positive emotion , such as happiness. Thus, it causes people (staffs) lack motivated reasoning to unconsciously evaluate evidence in ways consistent with whose preferences. This type of bias can hinder a company's ability to learn from mistakes and to build successful strategies."

However, Disney chose to implement knowledge management strategy to satisfy visitors demands and needs to let who feel more satisfactory when who entered Disney to play its any entertainment as below:

For first example, Disney demanded cleaners to repeat to remember any information to prepare to answer visitors' enquiries. It will train every cleaner memory to remember any information to be long term from short term memory successfully and every cleaner won't feel bore to do only cleaning job duty. When every one feel places are clean, who will concentrate on answering any visitors enquiries as the same time. Even, if they can give excellent service performance to serve visitors to let who to know how to go to any places in the short time. It is possible that visitors will appreciate whose service performance to let their manager to know, so that every cleaner will have chance to raise salary.

Besides for second example, waiting time and queues are daily problem for Disney theme park. Fast lines or priority queues appear as a solution of efficient queues for clients. Disney understood fast ticket line system affected visitor attendance numbers. Disney entertainment facilities long waits leaded to lower service evaluations and greater customer dissatisfaction. Efficient queue waiting time management can improve Disney visitor satisfaction and the willingness to recommend the service. Disney analysed of theme park visitor behaviour in relation to pay the higher ticket price to select to pay more for fast queuing line ticket than common queuing line ticket. In fact, Disney fast queuing line ticket system choice gave potential queues to any waiting clients . In general, Disney visitors don't like to wait long time in every entertainment facilities queuing line, who will feel a waste of time and waiting can lead to negative emotional response like frustration, impotence, tension or irritation .

In fact, Disney amusement theme park needed visitors wait long queues and delays which were a frequent occurrence in every entertainment facilities line. Disney theme park as sets of rides, spectacles and leisure mechanisms are intended to entertainment and spark the imagination of clients, allowing visitors to escape their daily routing. In result, waiting is often a problematic issue that can influence Disney visitor experience and that can appear as one of the principal motives for complaining. As Disney visitor demand fluctuates constantly and demand patterns are often difficult to predict. It caused extra staff needed for the extra line. Finally, priority services such as fast line system facilities segmentation of its amusement park. When Disney offer the possibility of purchases a fast line, which are creating two different group. Disney visitors who are highly sensitive to waiting times are willing to pay to avoid or reduce lines or visitors that are highly sensitive to price that prefer to wait rather than to pay extra money. Also, Disney provides extensive training opportunity for participants through its own Disney university. The question of whether their training opportunity can lead the improve human resource activities. On the third hand problem, Disney are also worried that employees may leave it and join other competitor to serve their parks after training. Disney shows a trend of increasing depending on human capital other than physical capital.

It thinks human capital is the knowledge, skills, ideas and commitment of its employees. It explains that investing in training and development is essential to its client service growth. In fact, Disney had owned enough entertainment facilities, restaurants, hotels, shopping centres within theme park, but its visitor numbers are increasing to need to be served satisfactorily. However, it needs to train cleaners, entertainment facilities service staffs, queuing service staffs, hotels, restaurants, shopping centres service staffs, instead of it's entertainment facilities attraction.

For the final example, Disney observes that spending on training and development is typically regarded as consumption, instead of investment. On job training usually can't be replaced by formal education, therefore Disney chooses to make contribution on providing further training and development to employees. Disney paid salary for staff training, which included classroom, seminars, symposia or conferences; computer based training, on site training, book and periodicals reading, formal mentoring and informal mentoring program opportunities to meet its old staffs and new staffs both needs of motivate factors to achieve advancement , achievement, personal growth responsibility and achievement and recognition to raise its business performance effectively and efficiently.

However, Disney's amount of training has a positive influence on intrinsic motivation of its employees. Job satisfaction, salary, working condition, its policies, administration, relationship with supervisors, peers and subordinates are Disney factors to influence it's human resource activities performance. Disney training contents include these functional area: Raising excellent service performance include that hotel food and beverage service delivery, shopping center, merchandise sale, restaurant service, entertainment facilities queuing waiting service, cleaning and enquiring how to go different locations in Disney, cashier service etc. They are very important to influence visitor numbers. Disney implementation of knowledge management solution to improve queuing waiting line process. The use of Disney front line service staffs as human capital combined with knowledge of customer preference has made the fast pass an innovation solution to enhance queuing in the Disney theme parks. Disney ability to capture customers in virtual queues when giving them a pleasurable waiting experience has made them a leader in knowledge management initiatives in the service industry. Disney's emphasis on human capital within their theme parks, combined with traditional queuing theory to create more pleasurable waiting environments. Hence, Disney showed the value of tacit employee knowledge integrated with traditional queuing theory to reduce loss of customer satisfaction to enhance, goodwill and profitability. Knowledge management expresses itself as human action in form of evaluation, attitudes, points of view, commitments, motivation etc. It seemed that Disney agreed that human capital (people, knowledge, ideas, creativity) maybe today's most valuable commodity.

How to apply knowledge management strategy to solve Disney long time queue waiting playing challenges? Knowledge Management Strategy was used to queue control from Disney. Disney managers have long understand the pressure of waiting time and revenue; who know that every minutes spent waiting in queuing is a minute that the client is not generating revenue. So, Disney managers have processed with design of a reservation system recognizes that guests can be freed from physically standing in the actually and perception of waiting by allowing guests to engage has arrived. Cope et al., (2008) showed that" the system was first tested at Disney in 1998. Managers assessed the system by surveying guests who used it. Results were positive and indicated that guests spent substantially less time in queuing, spent more per capita, and saw significantly more attractions, satisfaction level sky rocketed.The system was expanded in 1999 to include five of the most popular park attractions and was named FASTPASS. The system has since been expanded to all Disney theme parks worldwide, and is now in use by over 50 million guests per year .That guests have two options .Namely, they can choose to Obtain a FASTPASS ticket and come back a later, designed time or Wait in a traditional queuing. Guests are assisted in making their choice by information regarding estimated waits of both options. Thus, can decide to wait in the traditional queuing, or take a FASTPASS ticket and return it a later time with no further wait. Once an assigned FASTPASS time is generated and provided to a guest, it is valid for the 60 minutes beyond that time, creating a window in which guest can return."

There are numerous benefits in allowing park guests to return to an attraction within a designed time frame. Queue Waits involve managing two major client issues:

1.How long Disney visitors actually wait every time queue.

2.How long Disney visitor think they are waiting by whose psychological feeling every time queue.

Thus, if they feel that who spend much time to queue, it will cause they feel angry and they also feel admission ticket price is paid too high to them unfairly. In general, clients were allowed the ability to see two attractions during the time they would have previously been able to see only one. This can viewed as an implementation of a multi-phased system, depending on the attraction picked, each queuing may be single channel attractions, the guest creates whose own multi phase system. Obvious, results, were that guests were able to engage in more revenue producing activities, saw more of the popular attractions and began to par take care, in other less utilized attractions .

Wiig defined(1993)" Knowledge management in different ways and from different perspective. The emphasis is on human know how and how it brings value to an organization. Intangible asset contributes to corporation objective may be immeasurable and isn't simple to evaluate the impacts of knowledge management."

However, Knowledge management may not be only factor influencing organizational performance. In fact, Disney refined technology utilization to improve the user design of all human resource related systems, improving timeliness (queue waiting time deduction), setting elapsed time goals and monitor performance towards those standards, considering to use of automated fast queue waiting system, evaluating staffing levels, a close examination of adequacy of current staff level is warranted, beyond to improve visitors satisfaction. Clients holding fast pass tickets may choose to visit a gift shop or any park concessions. Thus, Disney has ability to co-branded products and service.

Disney's approach combining queuing and human capital. Dunn, J et al., (2002) showed "The use of fast pass provides an insightful application of the combination of techniques of queuing and human capital to strategically leverage knowledge management principle .When waiting lines are an part of the Disney experience, park guests build magical memories through innovation. It is Disney's recognition of front line service staffs that transforms that employees into knowledge who multi task in their roles. For example, an attraction host or a street sweeper may be a valuable Source knowledge to park guests. In addition to their primary roles, they may have a wealth of information about attractions for guests. They may be able to give directions, provide schedules, and offer helpful suggestions from their daily observation. This is the first stop to increase knowledge management . Next, Disney improves its clients' perception by minimizing the perception of waits. The use of the fast pass enables Disney not only to enhance the psychological aspect of waiting lines, but also to capitalize at the same time." Instead, Disney needed to give people specific tools designed to help them to do their job and solve specific business problems. Thus, after Disney learned how it applied the knowledge management method to solve its challenges, e.g. Human capital and queuing theory provide two very different valuable assets to raise its competitive ability. Then, its visitor numbers was increasing largely and quickly.

In conclusion, Disney need to change it's strategy to adapt any the business environmental situation change in different time. For example, in the past, due to Disney had encountered operation challenge and human resource management challenge. So, it apply fast queue knowledge management strategy to solve visitors' spending long queue time is needed to wait to play any Disney entertainment facilities to let them feel satisfactory and feel no angry to compaint Disney. It seems that it is more successful to attract many visitors prefer to pay admission fee to visit Disney to play.

However, nowaday, Disney is encountering another kind of challenge, such as how to let visitors feel that they can spend long time to enjoy any long time and expensive similar entertainment feeling, such as sitting rockets to fly to moon travel feeling. I shall recommend that it can apply space tourism strategy to design its entertainment facilities are similar to space tourism entertainment facilities to let its visitors feel that they can spend short time to sit rockets to travel to moon.

Can Disney short time knowledge management strategy solve long time queue entertainment waiting challenge to visitors ?

As Harriet Griffey (2010) stated that "sometimes, boredom can give disadvantages to reduce staffs' ability to motive to work and reduces positive emotion , such as happiness. Thus, it causes people (staffs) lack motivated reasoning to unconsciously evaluate evidence in ways consistent with whose preferences. This type of bias can hinder a company's ability to learn from mistakes and to build successful strategies." However, Disney needed to implement knowledge management strategy to satisfy visitors demand after who entered .Disney demanded cleaners to repeat to remember any information to prepare to answer visitors' enquiries. It will train every cleaner memory to remember any information to be long term from short term memory successfully and every cleaner won't feel bore to do only cleaning job duty. When every one feel places are clean, who will concentrate on answering any visitors enquiries as the same time. Even, if they can give excellent service performance to serve visitors to let who to know how to go to any places in the short time. It is possible that visitors will appreciate whose service performance to let their manager to know, so that every cleaner will have chance to raise salary. Besides, waiting time and queues are daily problem for Disney theme park. Fast lines or priority queues appear as a solution of efficient queues for clients. Disney understood fast ticket line system affected visitor attendance numbers. Disney entertainment facilities long waits leaded to lower service evaluations and greater customer dissatisfaction. Efficient queue waiting time management can improve Disney visitor satisfaction and the willingness to recommend the service. Disney analysed of theme park visitor behaviour in relation to pay the higher ticket price to select to pay more for fast queuing line ticket than common queuing line ticket. In fact, Disney fast queuing line ticket system choice gave potential queues to any waiting clients . In general, Disney visitors don't like to wait long time in every entertainment facilities queuing line, who will feel a waste of time and waiting can lead to negative emotional response like frustration, impotence, tension or irritation .In fact, Disney amusement theme park needed visitors wait long queues and delays which were a frequent occurrence in every entertainment facilities line. Disney theme park as sets of rides, spectacles and leisure mechanisms are intended to entertainment and spark the imagination of clients, allowing visitors to escape their daily routing. In result, waiting is often a problematic issue that can influence Disney visitor experience and that can appear as one of the principal motives for complaining. As Disney visitor demand fluctuates constantly and demand patterns are often difficult to predict. It caused extra staff needed for the extra line. Finally, priority services such as fast line system facilities segmentation of its amusement park. When Disney offer the possibility of purchases a fast line, which are creating two different group. Disney visitors who are highly sensitive to waiting times are willing to pay to avoid or reduce lines or visitors that are highly sensitive to price that prefer to wait rather than to pay extra money. Also, Disney provides extensive training opportunity for participants through its own Disney university. The question of whether their training opportunity can lead the improve human resource activities. On the third hand problem, Disney are also worried that employees may leave it and join other competitor to serve their parks after training. Disney shows a trend of increasing depending on human capital other than physical capital. It thinks human capital is the knowledge, skills, ideas and commitment of its employees. It explains that investing in training and development is essential to its client service growth. In fact, Disney had owned enough entertainment facilities, restaurants, hotels, shopping centres within theme park, but its visitor numbers are increasing to need to be served satisfactorily. However, it needs to train cleaners, entertainment facilities service staffs, queuing service staffs, hotels, restaurants, shopping centres service staffs, instead of it's entertainment facilities attraction.

Disney observes that spending on training and development is typically regarded as consumption, instead of investment. On job training usually can't be replaced by formal education, therefore Disney chooses to make contribution on providing further training and development to employees. Disney paid salary for staff training, which included classroom, seminars, symposia or conferences; computer based training, on site training, book and periodicals reading, formal mentoring and informal mentoring program opportunities to meet its old staffs and new staffs both needs of motivate factors to achieve advancement , achievement, personal growth responsibility and achievement and recognition to raise its business performance effectively and efficiently. However, Disney's amount of training has a positive influence on intrinsic motivation of its employees. Job satisfaction, salary, working condition, its policies, administration, relationship with supervisors, peers and subordinates are Disney factors to influence it's human resource activities performance. Disney training contents include these functional area: Raising excellent service performance include that hotel food and beverage service delivery, shopping center, merchandise sale, restaurant service, entertainment facilities queuing waiting service, cleaning and enquiring how to go different locations in Disney, cashier service etc. They are very important to influence visitor numbers. Disney implementation of knowledge management solution to improve queuing waiting line process. The use of Disney front line service staffs as human capital combined with knowledge of customer preference has made the fast pass an innovation solution to enhance queuing in the Disney theme parks. Disney ability to capture customers in virtual queues when giving them a pleasurable waiting experience has made them a leader in knowledge management initiatives in the service industry. Disney's emphasis on human capital within their theme parks, combined with traditional queuing theory to create more pleasurable waiting environments. Hence, Disney showed the value of tacit employee knowledge integrated with traditional queuing theory to reduce loss of customer satisfaction to enhance, goodwill and profitability. Knowledge management expresses itself as human action in form of evaluation, attitudes, points of view, commitments, motivation etc. It seemed that Disney agreed that human capital (people, knowledge, ideas, creativity) maybe today's most valuable commodity.

Bibliography

Ansoff, H.I. (1987) Corporate Strategy. Penguin, London

Bahandin, G. & Guerganna, K.S. United States, (Jan. 2009).Strategic human resource management and global expansion lessons from the Euro Disney challenges in France. International business & economics research journal, vol. 8, no.1.

Barnard, Bruce: Business is booming in the world's biggest tourist market, March 1999, p.22, Journal of Commerce, Brucells.

Barnard, Bruce: Business is booming in the world's biggest tourist market, March 1999a, p.24, Journal of Commerce, Brucells.

Benesch, Dieter, 1989: " Theme parks in Florida-Eine Analyse von Angebot und Nachfrage sowie Regionalwirtschaftfliche Auswirkungen" , Master 's Thesis at the University of Economics and Business Administration, Vienna. AAdvisor: Prof. Dr. Karl Sinnhuber, Library.

Brennan, L. & Vecchi, A., (2011). The Business Of Space, The Next Frontier Of International Competition. Palgrave Macmillan Press: USA, New York.

Charles B. (2012) Curiosity Takes Us Back to Mars the WHITE HOUSE Available at: Date Of Publication: 6 Aug. https://www.whitehouse.gov/blog/2012/08/06/curiosity-takes-us-back-mars

Cope, R. R. Cope and H. Davis (2008). Disney's virtual Queues: A strategic opportunity to co-brand services ? Journal of Business & economics research, vol. 6 no10, 13-20.

Dickson, D., R. Ford and B. Laval (2005). Managing real and virtual waits in hospitality and service organizations. Corncell hotel and restaurant administration quarterly, vol. 45 no1, 52-68.

Dunn, J & A Neumsister (2002). Knowledge management in the Information age. E. business review, Fall , 37-45. Jounral of service, spring

2011, vol. 4, no1, De Grovte (2009).

Edinger Tourismberatung GmbH: Study: "Die Entwickling von Freizeitparks in Osterreich, 1998, for: Bundeministerium fur wirtschaftliche Angelegenheiten, wien" Innsbruck.

ERA (Economics Research Associates) 1998: " The Future Role of Theme parks in International Tourism" , Clive B. Jones & John Robinett, Los Angeles, p.5

ERA (Economics Research Associates) 1998a: " The Future Role of Theme parks in International Tourism" , Clive B. Jones & John Robinett, Los Angeles, p.13

Foden, harry G. 1996, " Destination attractions as an economic development generator", Economic Development Review, Fall 1996, 10., American Economic Development council

Friedmann, David:" Status Report of the Los Angeles County Economy", Vol.1, prepared for the "Los Angeles Board of Commerce, 1999.p.78

Futron Corporation (2009) Resource Centre. Available at:http://www.futron.com/resource_centre/resource_cemtre.htm.

Gartrell, R.B. (1994) Destination Marketing for Convention and Marketing Bureaus. Kendall/Hunt Publishing, Dubuque, Iowa

Harriet Griffey. (2010) The art of concentration, enhance focus, Reduce, stress and achieve move. Macmillan publishers ltd,Basinastoke and Oxford, London UK.

Hertzfeld, H.R. (2007) Globalization, Commercial Space And Space Power In the USA, Space Policy, Vol.32, no 4. November.

IAAPA: International Accociation of Amusement Parks and Attractions (http://www.iaapa.prg), " Theme Park Industry at-a-a glance" (Brochure), 1999, Atlanta, Georgia.

Kotler, P., Bowen, J. and Makens, J (2003) Marketing for Hospitality and Tourism. Prentice Hall ?Pearson Education, New Jersey

Kotler. P., Hamlin, M.A., Rein, I. and Haider, D.H (2002) Marketing Asian Places: attracting investment, industry, and tourism to cities, states & nations. John Wiley & Sons (Asia) Pte. Ltd., Singapore

Kotler, P., Haider, D.H. and Rein, I (1993) Place Marketing. Free Press, New York

Kyriazi, Gary, "Amusement Parks: A Pictorial History" Secaucus, NJ: Castle Booka, 1997.

Lundberg, Donals E. (ph.D.): " The Tourist Business", 1995, 5. Edition- Published by Van Nostrand Reinhold Company, New York.

Middleton, V.T.C. & Clarke, J. (2001) Marketing in Travel & Tourism. Butterworth Heinemann, Oxford

PKF consulting, 1997: " Study of the Projected Future Tax for: The City of Anadheim, the Anaheim Public Financing Authority, Nov. 13, Collections From Designated Sources to be Received by the city of Anaheim", 1997, prepared -1997.

Tarasenko, M.V. (1996) Evolution Of The Soviet Space Industry, Acta Astronautica, Vol. 38, no. 4-8, pp. 667-73.

The Economist 1997: "The Los Angeles economy: Bigger than South Korea", Feb, 4. 1997 page 25-26, London.

Wiig, k.(1993). Knowledge management foundations: Thinking About thinking. How people and organizations create, represent and use knowledge vol.1 , of knowledge management series schema press: Arlington, TX.

Yip, GS. (2003) Total Global Strategy II: Updated For The Internet And Service Era (Upper Saddle River, NT: Presentice-Hall).

www.ingramcontent.com/pod-product-compliance
Ingram Content Group UK Ltd.
Pitfield, Milton Keynes, MK11 3LW, UK
UKHW021909190726
13853UKWH00002B/596